MW00824813

JAPANESE SWORD FIGHTING

JAPANESE SWORD FIGHTING

Secrets of the Samurai

MASAAKI HATSUMI

PHOTOS BY Minoru Hirata and Kyuzo Akashi

TRANSLATED BY Bruce Appleby and Doug Wilson

KODANSHA INTERNATIONAL
Tokyo · New York · London

NOTE FROM THE PUBLISHER:

This book is presented only as a means of preserving a unique aspect of the heritage of the martial arts. Neither the publisher nor the author makes any representation, warranty, or guarantee that the techniques described or illustrated in it will be safe or effective in any self-defense situation or otherwise. Readers may be injured if they apply or train in the techniques illustrated. To minimize the risk of injury, nothing described in this book should be undertaken without personal and expert instruction. In addition, a physician should be consulted before deciding whether to attempt any of the techniques described. Federal, state, or local law may prohibit the use or the possession of any of the weapons described or illustrated in this book. Specific self-defense responses illustrated in these pages may not be justified in any particular situation or applicable under federal, state, or local law. Neither the publisher nor the author makes any representation or warranty regarding the legality or appropriateness of any weapon or technique mentioned in this book.

The names of modern and contemporary Japanese appear in the Western order, while those of historical figures (pre–1868) are written in the traditional order: surname preceding given name.

For reference, the following chart shows those periods of Japanese history which will be most relevant to the discussion.

PERIOD NAME	APPROXIMATE DATES (A.D.)
Nara	710–784
Heian	794–1192
Kamakura	1192–1333
Muromachi	1336–1573
Nanbokucho	1336–1392
Sengoku	1467–1568
Azuchi-Momoyama	1573–1600
Edo	1600–1868
Meiji	1868–1912
Taisho	1912–1926
Showa	1926–1989
Heisei	1989–

(Historians do not agree on exactly when the various periods started and ended, so the dates listed are approximate. Japanese writing often refers as well to nengo, or shorter periods named after each reigning emperor. Some of these will be introduced where relevant.)

Photos (pp. 64–65, upper) by Isabel Benchetrit.

Distributed in the United States by Kodansha America, Inc., and in the United Kingdom and continental Europe by Kodansha Europe Ltd.

Published by Kodansha International Ltd., 17-14 Otowa 1-chome, Bunkyo-ku, Tokyo 112-8652, and Kodansha America, Inc.

Copyright © 2005 by Masaaki Hatsumi and Kodansha International Ltd.
Translation copyright © 2005 by Bruce Appleby and Doug Wilson.
All rights reserved. Printed in Japan.
ISBN 978-4-7700-2198-4

First edition, 2005
15 14 13 12 11 10 09 08 07   10 9 8 7 6 5 4 3

www.kodansha-intl.com

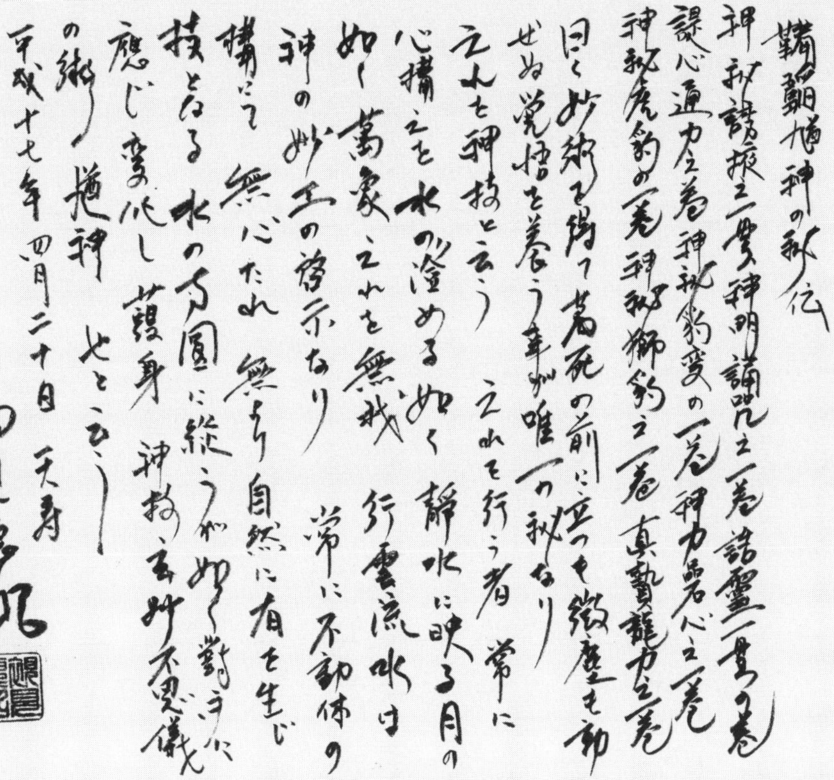

鞨鞨楯神の神伝

押取諸技二雲神明諸兜立一巻　諸霊一雲之巻
誤心通力之善神祝豹変の一巻　神力君心之巻
神祝虎豹の一巻　神祝獅豹之一巻　真勁龍力之巻

曰く妙術を得て萬死の前に立つて微塵も動
せぬ覚悟を善う事如唯一の秘なり
立れを神技と云う　立れを行う者　常に
心構えを　水の澄める如く　静水に映る月の
如く　萬象　立れを無我　行雲流水け
神の妙工の啓示なり　常に不動体の
構にて　無心たれ　無より自然に有を生じ
技となる　水の方圓に従うが如く　對う心に
應じ変化し　護身　神技玄妙不覚儀ん
の術　揺神　七と二し一

平成十七年　四月二十日　天寿

初見良昭
白龍翁　筆

CONTENTS

CHAPTER 3   The Practice of Budo

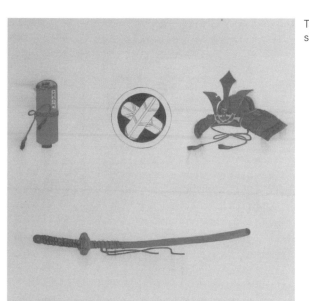

Bishamonten and Kabutowari (also called Hachi-wari) worn by the military commander Kusunoki Masashige. It says "Kusunoki Tamon Hyoue Masashige" in the signature.

神霊雷火一心神力

尊氏公

足利殿正三位権大納言征夷大将軍治天下二十五年

義詮 尊氏公嫡男正二位権大納言

尾刃名時女相別感時御煉之

仁一位大臣鵰位官尊氏公御臺所

深義徳 仁一位大臣御方

源義持公 義詮御方

仁一位大后 義満御子

従位信左衛新将源義重 勁雪車小路新投殿

榮雨刀

帯雨刀

夢沙陰満 扇 語言

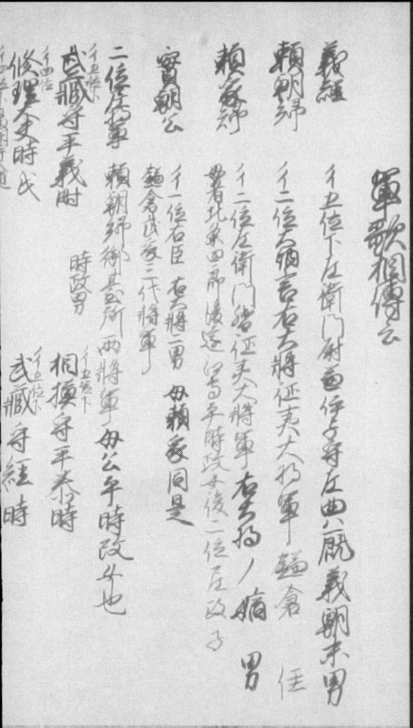

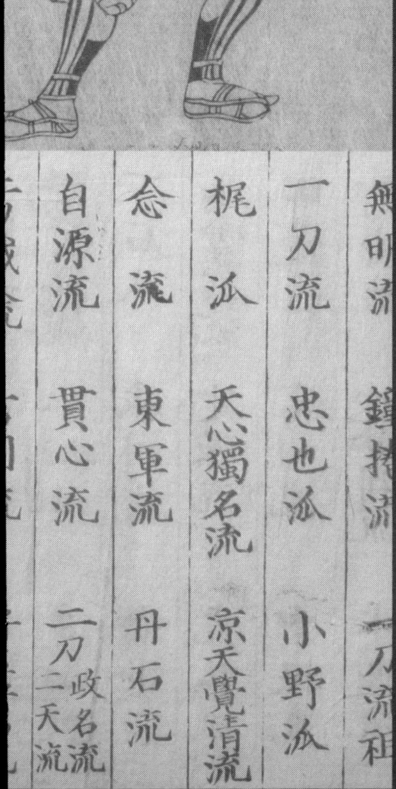

心気風雲神通力

軍歌相傳云

義經
頼朝卿
頼義卿
宮賴公

二位尼公
武藏守平義附
後醍醐安時氏
武藏守經時

無明流	鐘捲流	一刀流祖
一刀流	忠也派	小野派
梶派	天心獨名流	京天覽清流
念流	東軍流	丹石流
自源流	貫心流	二刀政名流 二刀二天流

増念覚刀大水客所力

Eight-boat leaping by Minamoto-no Yoshitsune.

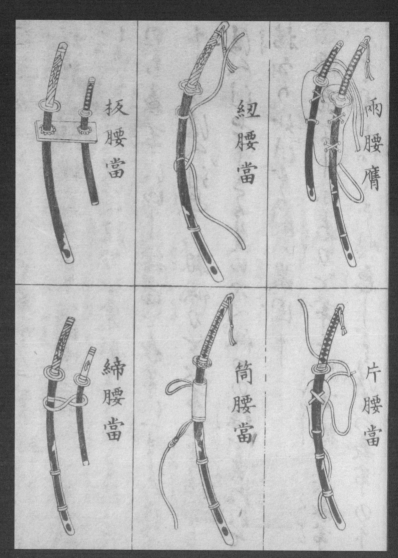

扳腰當　紐腰當　兩腰膺

締腰當　筒腰當　片腰當

A selection of koshiate (sword-attaching to the waist.)

PREFACE

In Honor of True Warriors

There is a word in Japanese, 'kensei 劍聖,' meaning 'sword saint.' Sword saints are different from sword experts or sword masters. Sword masters were individuals such as Iizasa Choisai, Aisu Ikosai, Koizumi Isenokami, Tsukahara Bokuden, Yagyu Sekishusai, Miyamoto Musashi, and Ito Ittosai. Historical records are replete with tales of these undefeated sword masters; their sword skills were said to be divine, and their fame still echos to the present day. Tomita Shigemasa distinguished himself in service while serving three generations of the lord Maeda and rose in rank to receive 13,000 koku of rice, while Yagyu Munenori, the master of Shinkage-ryu, only received 12,500 koku (koku was a measure of rice paid as currency). The Chinese character for 'koku' (石) is written with the character for 'stone' (石). In relation to this, the great leader of the Warring States period (1467–1568), Takeda Shingen, once famously said "people are stone." Koku, or 'stones,' however, were a measure of rice, a salary to the samurai, but beyond this were a symbol of authority and a measure of economic status and military power. Munenori taught Shinkage-ryu to the shogun Tokugawa Hidetada for six years and became the head of the Shogun's intelligence service. Munenori was also renowned as a strategist and predicted the death in battle of Itakura Shigemasa, who was sent to suppress the Shimabara rebellion by the Shogunate. He had the 'consistent character' (kankaku, 貫格), rather than 'feeling' (kankaku, 感覚), of a martial artist (Budoka), excelling in the ability of foresight.

So, who were the sword saints? They were people who did not only excel in the way of fighting with the sword but had also reached a position that transcended the sword masters. Sword saints were also far superior to those who practiced the way of the sword in the dojo. Such lesser swordsmen had forgotten the sense of being able to respond in a life and death situation, and lacked experience that was useful in real combat. When we consider it, most sword masters were born in the period between the end of the Warring States period and the time

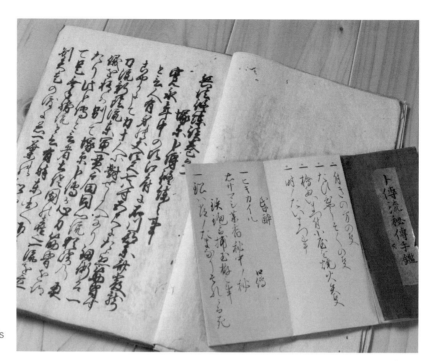

Tsukahara Bokuden and his densho.

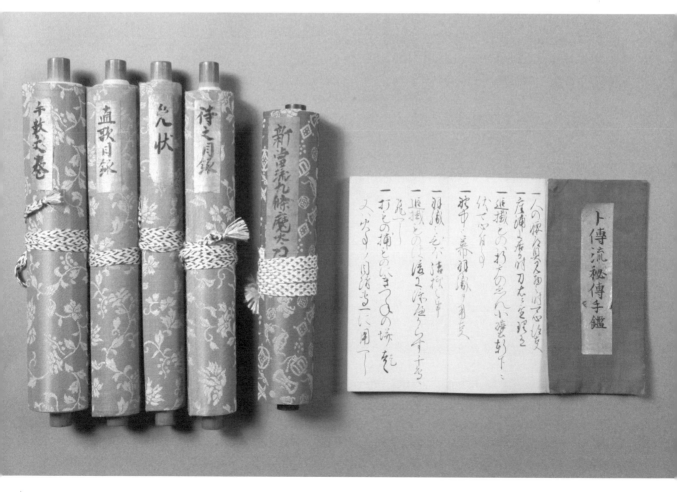

when guns began to appear on the battlefield. The sword saints, on the other hand, began to appear in times of war (toso, 闘争) that were the time of sword and spear (toso, 刀槍); a much earlier period.

Yet it is only those that by good fortune survived and won fame and status as sword masters who are now remembered. Accepting, however, that only these people should be remembered as sword masters, we lose sight of the sword saints. Although the names of some sword saints have disappeared, they were great individuals who had real power, comparable to those who managed to make a name for themselves. For that reason, I am writing this book to honor the memory of these forgotten sword saints.

Takamatsu Toshitsugu Sensei once said, "Even if some are called masters, how many other masters were there?" To evaluate a soldier by whether they were strong or whether they won a fight is a mundane and practical pursuit; the demeanor of the warriors known as sword saints has a beauty that resembles nature itself: snow, the moon, and flowers.

Memories of the time I was taught the Budo of the nine schools by Takamatsu Sensei are like flashes of a dream that appear as profound images of transmission (kaden, 家伝) or mist (kaden, 霞伝).

This is the transmission of old soke (head of a school) to new soke; the transition of teacher to student. That path could also be called the path of truth in nature. Masters and experts appear to shine like glittering stars. However, the path of the sword saints, like the passing of days from sun to moon, shows its color to both master and student. That color appears in five shades, which correspond to the five guiding principles of the essence of Budo and Ninjutsu:

1. Learn first that whatever hardship you may have to endure is but temporary.

2. Always behave correctly.

3. Do not fall pray to avarice, indulgence, or egoism.

4. Sorrow and hate are both part of life; understand that they too are gifts from the gods.

5. Never stray from the path of faith nor from that of martial arts. Aspire in the ways of both pen and sword.

Picture of the battle of Kawanakajima.

If you have the eyes to see the character 'to aspire' (志) is comprised of the characters for 'warrior' (士) and 'heart' (心), then you can interpret the benevolent heart of the warrior who presents a gift of condolence at a funeral ceremony with the feeling of reverence for the Buddha, and the verse: "The way of Bushi is found in death." Furthermore, you will understand the mercy of the suicide assistant at a seppuku ceremony. If you wish to walk the path of the sword saint, I urge you to preserve this motto in your mind, and walk the path steadily with bufu ich-igei (mastery of one talent in the martial ways).

CHAPTER 1

Kenpo in Budo

True understanding of real Budoka

It is taken for granted that swords cut well. However, there are cases when the opponent is wearing armor that the sword will not cut as expected. Around the end of the Warring States period, it was decreed by the emperor that non-samurai would be disarmed and their swords taken away in programs of weapons confiscation known as 'katanagari.' As encapsulated in the expression "The pen is mightier than the sword," culture superseded fighting, and an age of enlightenment ensued. Swords survived as beautiful works of art, but swordsmen continued to diminish. It is difficult to appreciate the profound impact of this decree without having lived in a time when swords were actually used and formed an integral part of society. Indeed, our true understanding of real Budoka

Kumamoto Castle. ▶

is also limited in our modern age. So, in order to understand real Budo, let us take a trip back to the Muromachi period (1336–1573), the peak of swordsmanship that started with Koizumi Isenokami and Tsukahara Bokuden, sword masters who emerged in this period.

Warriors who lived at this time discovered the relative merits of the tachi and the associated techniques of cutting, thrusting, and striking while engaging in combat (Kumiuchi). Firstly, it is important for us to understand that Kenpo was born from this era, and furthermore understand that martial arts came from combat that did not rely upon the sword.

From the time of the Northern and Southern Dynasties (1336–92) to the Muromachi period up to the Warring States period, in an era characterized by the trend for retainers to supplant their lords, the flower of Bushido was pollinated and blossomed, it scattered in the wind and then bloomed again in the month of the warrior (shigatsu, 士月)—April (shigatsu, 四月).

This process can be likened to the life of a salmon. Salmon face a strong current and climb up river to fertilize. They lay their eggs and, while continuing to fight, die. From this the fate of the next generation can be seen. This corresponds with the form of the warriors who died, fighting to maintain the honor of their family and descendents year after year. This destiny, born in the Muromachi period, most beautifully expresses the world of the Bushi. The Muromachi period was the true starting point of the natural benevolence of the warrior. The period can be seen metaphorically as a flower. It was the era of the origin of Zen culture, Gozan literature, and the oneness of the sword and Zen—it was a period that moved away from the subtle and profound culture of Medieval times to a blossoming and flowering culture of arts and learning.

During the Muromachi period, the flower of Gozan literature was opened by the famous Zen

御子上典膳

傳流
一刀流
忠明

両傳合法

北辰一刀流開祖

千葉周作

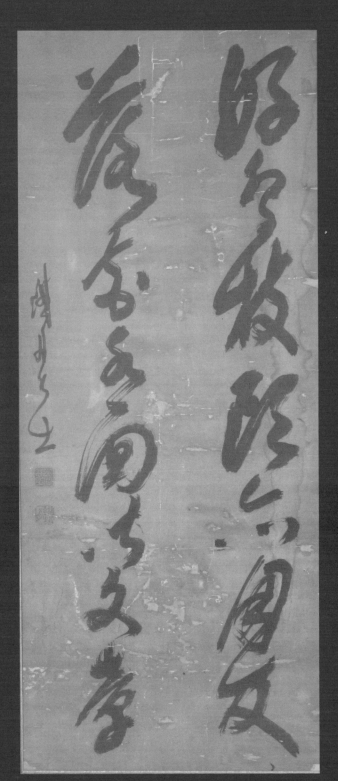

Writing by Yamaoka Tesshu.

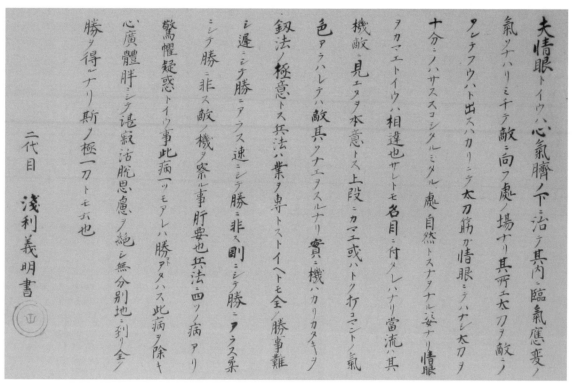

夫情眼トイウハ心氣臍ノ下ニ治テ其内ニ臨氣應変ノ
氣ツナハリミチテ敵ニ向フ處ヲ場ナリ其所エ太刀ヲ敵ヲ
アレテフウハト出スハカリニシテ太刀筋ガ情眼ニテハナシ太刀ヲ
十分ニノハサススコシノミタル處自然トスナヲナル姿ナリ情眼
ヲカマエトイウハ相違也サレトモ名目ニ付メレハナリ當流ハ其
機敵ニ見エヌヲ本意トス上段ニカマエ或ハトクカマントノ氣
色アラハレテハ敵其法ハ上ヲヲ專トストイヘトモ全ノ勝事難
釼法ノ極意トス其法ハ業ヲ專トスルナリ實ニ機ハカリカスキヲ
ニ遅ニシテ勝ニアラス速ニシテ勝ニ非ス剛ニシテ勝ヲアラス柔
ニシテ勝ニ非ス敵ノ機ヲ察ル事肝要也兵法ニ四ッ病アリ
驚懼疑惑トイウ事此病(一ツモアレハ勝アタハス此病ヲ除キ
心廣體胖ニシテ恬寂活脱思慮ヲ絶ニ無分別地ニ到リ全ノ
勝ヲ得ニナリ斯ノ極一刀トモ六也

二代目

浅利義明書

Writing by Asari Matashichiro Yoshiaki, teacher of Yamaoka Tesshu.

priests led by Ikkyu Sojun. At the same time Noh drama, the tea ceremony, and flower arrangement were born. These arts were able to develop under the patronage of the shogun and other powerful people. Nevertheless, at this time, artistic expression that opposed the power of the shogun was destroyed. For example, the famous Noh playwright Zeami was forced to live in exile on an island after falling out of favor with the shogun. I am often left wondering why Zeami did not perform the subtle and profound world he explained in his work *Fushikaden*, in which he famously said: "If it is hidden, it is the flower." The shogun would surely have admired it. It would seem that the soul of art and performance transcend the world of the living; there is a power in art that derives from the world of the dead. This kind of demonic spirit drives creativity and energetic, outstanding performances in the theater. It is a world untouched by those who are not artists, and feared by those who have power. This is why the revered tea ceremony master Sen no Rikyu, who possessed this demonic spirit, was killed by the powerful leader Toyotomi Hideyoshi, who feared him. Powerful people certainly feared the martial artists as well. However, a martial artist who protected the five rules and achieved enlightenment was truly a unique person. It is a matter of course, therefore, that the idea of the oneness of the sword

Tessen (iron fan) with a painting by Kano Hozui.

天文改悟三年頼川廿六日依之末
申寿院大唐渓但羽甲時
美祖文桐摸寺擢技道之
之依為他定一ヲ外者不傳
從放ハ外文改桐傳之者
右巷者先祖ヨリ持傳書之
小竹五原巷之内有
天文廿三年寅十二月日
五代目
道清
炮術秘書ニ八重者ハ

稲冨桐摸寺

傷冨一喜亥

Secret densho on Teppo (gun/rifle) by Inatomi Ichimu.

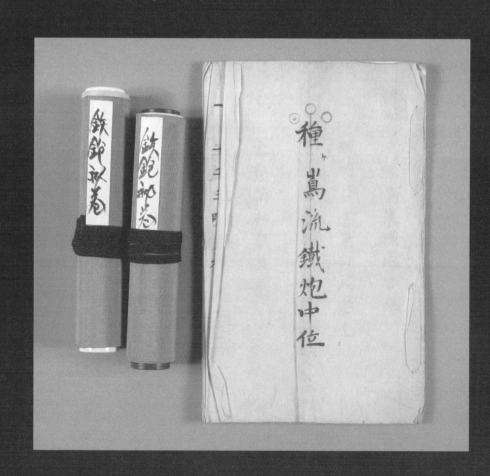

and Zen was born. Another meaning for 'Oni' (鬼, devil) in the realm of the dead is 'kami' (神, god). That is to say that the realm of the dead is irrevocably connected by a spiritual force to the world of the gods, and represents the divine world.

Divine Merit through the Peaceful Way of the Sword

Sakakibara Kenkichi was an active master swordsman from the end of the Edo period into the Meiji period (the mid to late 19th century). It is said that he was a master of Jikishinkage-ryu and was known for his technique of splitting the helmet. Though he was skilled at cutting a helmet in some small way, it is nevertheless strange to praise this as something significant. If you truly want to split a helmet, it is best that you smash it into many pieces using a large axe or halberd. A large axe, one of the seven elemental tools, will easily split a helmet—this is war strategy.

The five accompaniments of a sword are the deity within a Shinto shrine, respect, prayer, prosperity, and kiai (projection of the fighting spirit into a voice). These are all bound together, to make kami-musubi (binding with the gods). This also means that when you wield a sword, you should never cut a deity, but rather pray and pay your respects to the deity through the sword.

A well known master swordsman, and magnificent calligrapher who expressed the philosophy of the oneness of sword and Zen, was Yamaoka Tesshu (1836–88). Tesshu served for ten years in charge of the education of the Meiji Emperor. It is said that after he experienced rigorous training in the dojo, he eventually reached enlightenment, and was able to separate himself from his match with his teacher Asari Yoshiaki. Whereas Yoshiaki always used to win, Tesshu finally found enlightenment and beat him; finding the true meaning of victory and defeat and the way of the sword.

It should be understood that he realized enlightenment by hearing the poetic song of the gods in his heart. There is a song of the gokui (essence) that says: "In the world of martial arts, one should not stick to strength or weakness, softness or hardness; rather one should transcend physicality and understand the void, 'ku,' regarding the body also as empty." He was able to hear this song in a neutral, detached, Zen-like way. As a great ship in the vast ocean cuts through the waves, his eyes were opened to the gokui of the Itto-ryu, and he heard its rhyme. In war, prepare your body and show courage, the true gokui is the mind. Win without drawing your sword. If you draw, do not cut down; bear patiently, and know that taking a life is a grave thing.

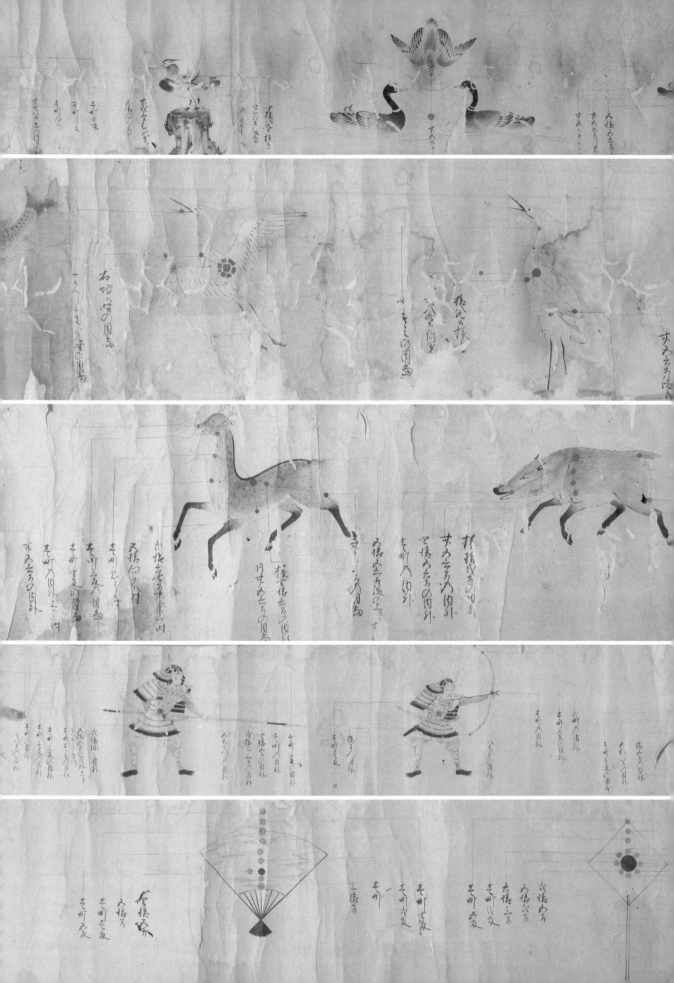

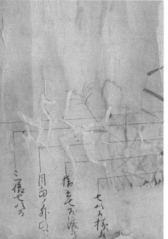

In the winter of 2004, several students and I were giving a demonstration of kami-mu cutting known as kami-musubi at the Kotohira Jinja grand festival in Noda City. Using the method of shihogiri (cutting all directions), two wara (sheaved straw) were cut completely through. However, the fifth wara for the kami-musubi was not allowed to be cut. When presenting to the gods, if all the wara are completely cut then it becomes an act of severing divine connection with the gods. Those watching who do not understand this may think the cutter was unable to sever the last wara. This is not the case. To revere the image of a Buddha in Zen (or kami in Shinto) to the point of idol-worship is wrong, and it is true that by destroying this very idol, one can achive enlightenment. True Budoka, however, will never fall prey to idol-worship, and so it is forbidden for them to cut the image of a Buddha even in a performance.

The Essence of Victory and Defeat

Within Budo, the ability to foresee certain victory is critical. Hesitation will not arise from a mind prepared for absolute victory. It is generally accepted that all people desire life. This aspect of fighting is expressed in old documents as "Koteki Ryoda Juppo Sessho no Jutsu," and in nature as the tiger fighting the dragon. The flash of lightning brings forth a thundercloud and a thunderstorm, the echo of wind grows louder, the aesthetic effect of fear rises. Stepping into this scene, your six senses are absorbed. Even if you yield victory to your opponent, in true Budo this should not be regarded as a bad thing. The ability to recognize defeat is important and essential to training in the martial arts. This is nothing more than a rule of nature, but those who indulge in lust or desire will never realize this. Let us just say that this is true to the style of author Nakazato Kaizan's endless cycles of rebirth, or give and take. However, what is critical here is that in real combat, victory or defeat is a matter of life or death. If you have the capacity to recognize defeat as also important, then your life force will be stronger, and this in turn cultivates courage with calmness.

Fights yield a winner and a loser. From the smallest thing, invincible people can be led to defeat. This becomes all the more apparent in a fight with real swords and not in the Dojo. Needless to say, strikes or thrusts with a shinai (bamboo sword), are not so serious, but if it is a real sword, they could be fatal. True warriors, however, will cultivate readiness without fear, regardless of whether they are in a duel with real swords or not. This is because they are standing on the lifeline of enlightenment; they are detached from victory or defeat, and have the insight and knowledge to separate themselves. This is part of the reverberation of life; of the essential five elements from *the Book of Five Rings*, which can be likened to the five lines on a musical score; the five ('go,' 五) of enlightenment ('go,' 悟). The musical score is written 'go sen fu' 五線符, as music on a page. In the same way, we can connect it to the five elements of enlightenment, 'go sen fu' 悟閃賦.

An acquaintance of mine who has trained with me for twenty years, and who was originally in the military of his country, recently wrote me a letter touching on the subject of the bloodshed of terrorism in the world around us: "As a person who has experienced actual combat, I'm certain that no matter what kind of war, no person is victorious, and I feel that in reality all are losers; even those who are victorious will suffer from the blood of the defeated enemy on their hands sooner or later." Those who yearn too much for victory suffer forever from their victory.

Is it possible that war between mankind will never end? The Ninja, fully understanding this possibility, devoted themselves to the gods, and in their shadow, the principle of 'shinmyoken' (mysterious sword) was born. Why is there conflict in life? If you were to change the four characters that make up the words 'natural selection' (shizen tota, 自然淘汰) to those of the phonetically identical 'nature's many battles' (shizen tota 自然闘多), you might think you were watching a dramatization of the mystery of the struggle for life.

Religion and Budo

There were approximately twenty types of primitive man, and of those, the hunter Cro-Magnon (Homo Sapiens), was the only one to survive. It is interesting, then, that the Cro-Magnon was the most frightened of the spirits of the dead. This deep natural mental state was probably a primitive version of the present day religious defensive reaction to death. If we accept the explanation that the only human to survive was Cro-Magnon because of their migration patterns, communication with words, fighting animals in groups, and superior hunting skills, then it can be said that modern man developed language competence, physical ability, society, and fighting instinct from his ancestors. Furthermore, it is because the Cro-Magnon were indeed a hunting people that they used weapons and traps. Natural selection is therefore an outcome of 'nature's many battles.'

The importance of Budo is seen here. Budo is to live. If your feelings are violent and brutal, then the way will be lost, but if the feeling is too humane, then you cannot hunt effectively. Already there is an excess of people on the globe. The world's current population of 6.4 billion

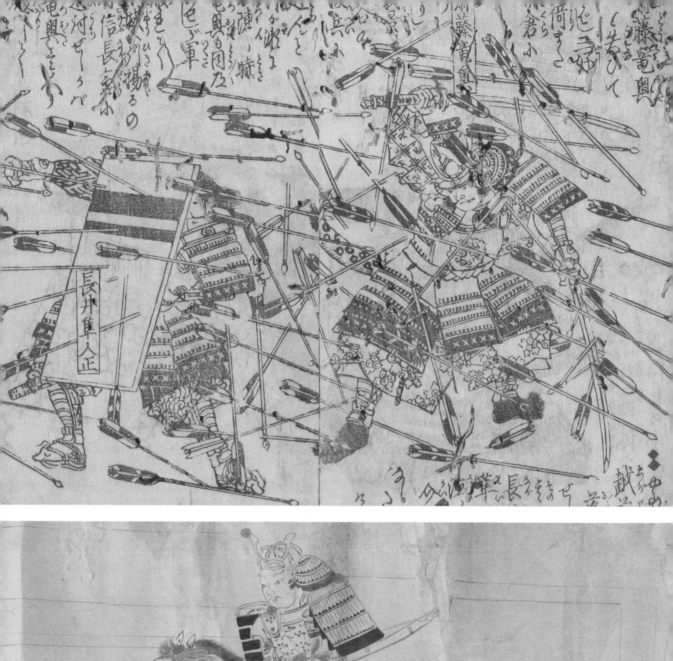

will increase to approximately 9.1 billion by the year 2050. We will also begin to see a transformation in the meaning of 'nature's many battles' to meteorological and geological phenomenon; a change in the phenomenon of natural battles.

My teacher Takamatsu Toshitsugu warned me that the occurrence of natural disasters such as earthquakes, volcanic eruptions, tsunamis, and floods are a revelation of the gods. The reason for these phenomena is the destruction of the earth's environment by man, and his lack of insight, perseverance, and understanding of the substance of nature. Therefore, to resent nature for its disasters, which we have helped create, would be pure hypocrisy.

Nature created the world in this way, and mankind is reaping the effects of his violation, so therefore such evils of mankind should be set right. This is the simple principle of give and take—if humankind does something good for nature, then nature will look after humankind and good things will come in return.

Currently, much is being said about global warming, but relying on a thermometer alone does not reveal the true extent of the crises of life. The thermometer (kandankei, 寒暖計) or intuition (kandankei, 寒断計) held by creatures of nature should be treated with more significance. Nature's creations continue to live bound by the ties of nature. The Shizen no Kamae (natural posture) in Budo is equal to this natural embodiment.

Thus, in Budo, as in nature, natural posture is important. From the old times it has been said that "the warrior heart is a reflection of harmony and respect." To say this in another way, Budoka are professors of the scientific ability to create the chemistry of change, having the feeling and ultra-conciousness of practitioners of religion, philosophers, and intellectuals. From the character for change (ka, 化) many other phonetic cousins are born—such as flower (ka, 花), shoe (ka, 靴), profit (ka, 貨), and to lean (ka, 傾). Ka is a puzzle in disguise. Sword saints strive to connect the expertise (ka, 家) of religion, philosophy, politics, and ideas.

War is often caused by conflict in religion, philosophy, and thought. Budo, however, must protect the 'Three spheres (ka, 家)' of religion, philosophy, and thought. Failure to do so would have severe consequences. Someday, this martial arts view will be regarded as very natural, just as

Densho of Saburi-ryu sojutsu. ▶

水月

水車

表裏

children's tales are. Nevertheless, even children's fairy tales, such as the Brothers Grimm collection, can be extremely frightening, and often hide something cruel. Mothers read them to their children often unaware of this. If we interpret these stories, however, with a protective instinct, we can notice the stories' cruel points.

The word 'cruelty' can be looked at in the flow of nature. With the right eyes you can see a rainbow in cruelty. There is a saying: "life is rosy," but there is also a blooming rose in the four natural stages of human life—birth, aging, sickness, and death; the rose blooms in all aspects of life. Regarding cruelty, the teachings of god are also very harsh in truth. And this is why in each age holy men appear. It is very interesting that Jesus Christ, Mohammed, and the Buddha appeared around the same period. Furthermore, Plato, Lao Tsu, and Confucius also lived in the period around that time. Times of reformation require great men.

What can we do in order to evade natural selection (many battles)? As in the song of the gokui, the art of not being an opponent to those that attack is probably the same principle of pacifism adovocated by Mahatma Gandhi.

After writing the book *The Way of the Ninja*, I received comments that it had assisted people in knowing the law of the way of the three powers—heaven, earth, and man—can be interpreted as culture, garden, and Ninja. Dry landscape gardens are one aspect of the perfection of culture in Japan. White sand creates mountains, rivers, oceans, and ponds expressing the beauty of nature in dry landscapes. However, unfortunately in present day Japan there are fewer and fewer homes with Japanese gardens. It requires more money than is generally realized to create and maintain a garden, which the average Japanese cannot afford. However, I must stress that it is only natural that developing, maintaining, and passing on culture is expensive. It is the Budoka that truly devote themselves to knowledge of the arts of culture. Thereby, one can take a philosophical view of life and death, victory and defeat. That is to say, to be a warrior who can reach wisdom (shiki, 識). Shiki has multiple meanings at the same time: to respect the manner of dying (shiki, 死悸), emphasize the importance of determination (shiki, 士気), as well as to revere the arts, and to have the aesthetic sense to protect tradition for eternity.

Oneness is infinite
Within Mikkyo (esoteric Buddhism), 'shiki' (wisdom) exists alongside the elements earth (chi, 地), water (sui, 水), fire (ka, 火), wind (fu, 風),

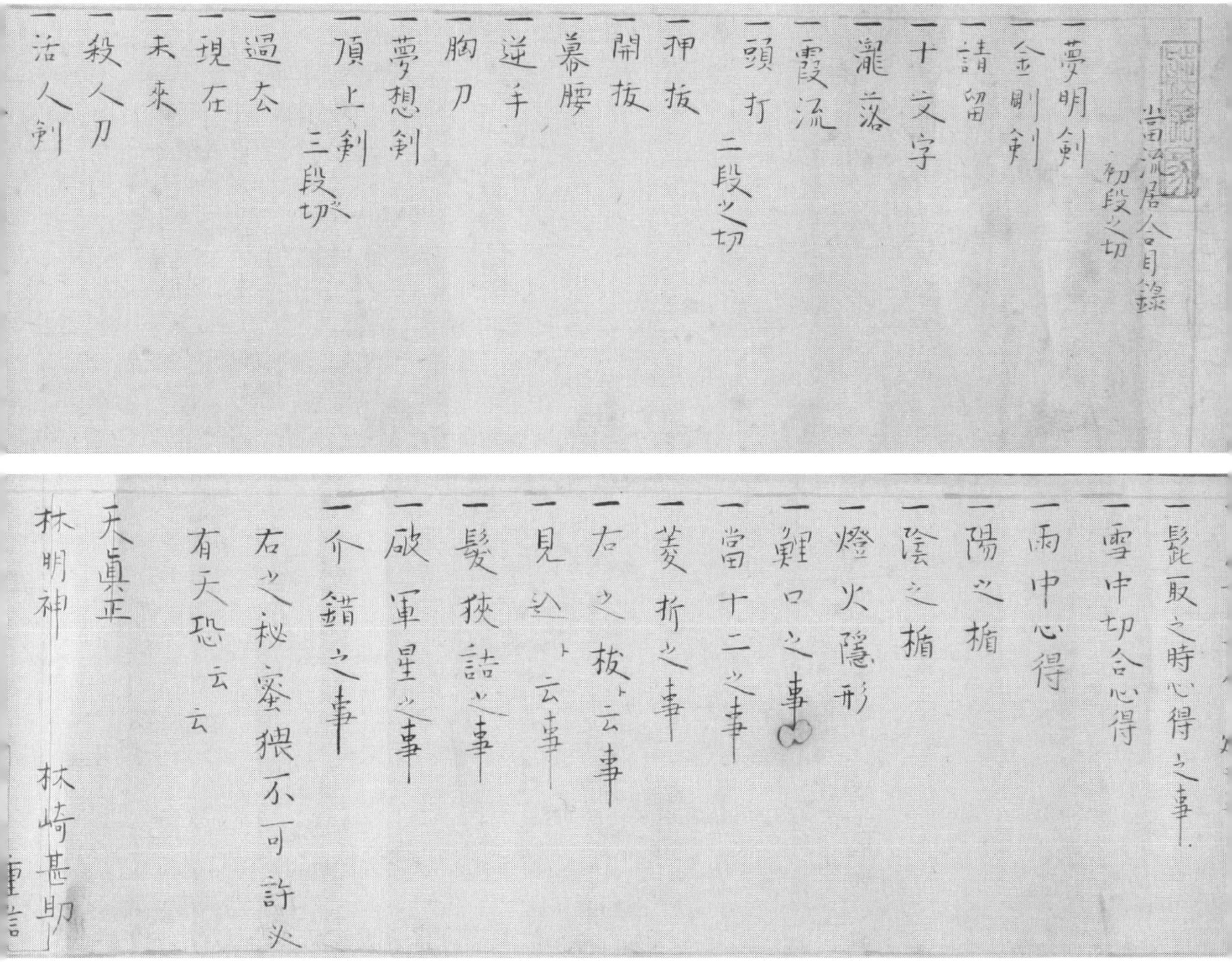

当流居合目録
初段之切

一 夢明剣
一 金剛剣
一 請留
一 十文字
一 瀧落
一 霞流
一 頭打　二段之切
一 押抜
一 開抜
一 幕腰
一 逆手
一 胸刀
一 夢想剣
一 頂上剣　三段切べ
一 過去
一 現在
一 未来
一 殺人刀
一 活人剣

一 髭ヲ取之時心得之事
一 雪中切合心得之事
一 雨中心得
一 陽之楯
一 陰之楯
一 燈火隠形
一 鯉口之事
一 当十二之事
一 菱折之事
一 右之抜ト云事
一 見込ト云事
一 髪狭詰之事
一 破軍星之事
一 介錯之事

右之秘密猥不可許火
有天恐云々

天真正
林明神
林崎甚助

Densho by Hayashizaki Jinsuke.

and emptiness (ku, 空). Shiki can also be read as the character for color (shiki, 色). Within Ninpo (the ways of the Ninja) it is said one must endure with conciousness (shiki) but you can also see the color of the mandala (portraits of mystic Buddhist symbols of the universe). The age of ink paintings has passed on to the age of color, and many mandala are now depicted in color. However, is it not said that in sumie (black ink painting) the sumi (black ink) has five subtle colors within it? Adding those five colors to the seven colors of the rainbow, we see twelve colors, corresponding to the months of the year. Thus we begin to see how years pass. The Noh song "Sotoba Komachi" equates the five rings (chi, sui, ka, fu, ku) to the human body. It is important to see the illusion of the five rings of Buddhism. It is said the Dutch painter Hulce managed to express no fewer than twenty-seven different colors with black, surely a mark of true genius.

Martial artists (strategists of war) look at things on a broad scale and carefully think about them. While all things in the universe have an ura (inside) and omote (outside), there is also the godai (the five elements) and rokudai (the six worlds, six virtues a Buddha elect practices to attain supreme enlightenment, and the six tools of the Ninja). Furthermore, there are the shichidai (the seven elements) and hachidai (the eight elements, within Budo known as the kihon happo). All these numbers have special importance. The world is thus complex and mysterious. In Buddhism there are six worlds of reincarnation. Beyond these there is the way of the rainbow—the seventh way—and because of this, the rainbow comes to symbolize the number seven. However, if you are imbued with that rainbow, then it becomes dangerous. This is because the number seven (shichi) in Japan is considered bad luck (it relates to the traditional 'seven hardships' of ancient Buddhism).

Picture of the warrior Imai Shiro Kanehira, a chief retainer of Kiso Yoshinaka.

Oneness extends to the infinite—this is an endless principle of Budo, but is not limited only to Budo. It also applies to religion and study. I do not subscribe to the belief that Budo is the ultimate phenomenon in the world at all. I feel that it is just one of many things that exist on this earth. There is a saying: "all things united as one." This is expressed in the symbol ⊖. In Zen this symbol represents hospitality. The great Buddhist monk Daruma was originally depicted in paintings realistically, but his image was progressively reduced to a symbol ○. Thus complex things come to be represented simply and symbolically. Daruma's symbol also means oneness and emptiness.

Densho of Kashima ▶
Shinden Kage-ryu.

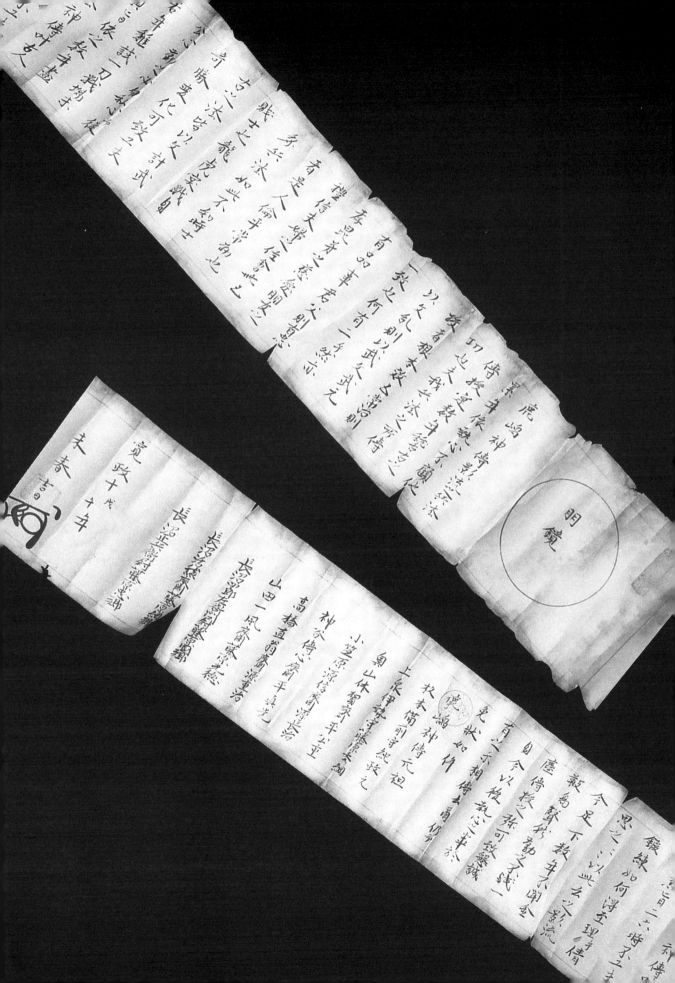

The real meaning of the eighteen fields of martial arts

Recently, I have been concerned about consistency (ikkan, 一貫), which is important in all the arts. My teacher Takamatsu Sensei told me forty-eight years ago, although it seems like only yesterday, that even an insect can go far if he grabs onto the tail of a horse. I replied, "There is a proverb that says a horse can go far; yet a Mongolian tiger travels far to hunt, but returns from 1,000 miles." Moko no Tora (Mongolian Tiger) was Takamatsu Sensei's martial nickname; indeed he was talented like the tiger.

Currently, I keep a horse called Cookie. I began painting a picture of a horse about ten years ago, and would often return to it to add some retouches, but I could never seem to appreciate it. However, after living with Cookie, I was able to complete the painting in a way with which I was satisfied.

There are two words: the kabuki juhachiban, and bugei juhachiban. These mean the 18 representative works of kabuki and the 18 basic fields of martial arts respectively. Speaking of the 18 fields of martial arts, the following disciplines come to mind: taijutsu, kenjutsu, bojutsu, sojutsu, iaijutsu, bajutsu, shurikenjutsu, and hobakujutsu (art of arresting). Here I would like to discuss the 18 works of kabuki through the eyes of a martial artist. In kabuki's heyday, Ichikawa Danjuro, Onoe Kikugoro, and Ichikawa Sadanji were renowned performers, and they dominated kabuki for a generation. 18 in this instance is when 3 people step in 6 directions; the number 18 harmonizes and the play becomes a charming martial performance. The number 18, which also means 'one's strength' in Japanese, relates to the idea of performing a great deed, including in battle.

The restoration of Budo

Life is an instant. Valuing life in the moment, as 'one encounter, one chance,' being grateful to divine providence that allows us to live in nature, loving the existence of everything in life, finding eternity in an instant—these are the profound and essential qualities of an artist. Luckily, we can find this kind of profound knowledge in the work of people who were able to enjoy fulfillment accumulated from the experience of life.

In the famous secret scrolls of Noh-drama *Fushikaden* by Zeami, it is written: "If it is hidden, it is the flower. If it is not hidden, it is not the flower." By suppressing and concealing the intention, one can stimulate the imagination. It is very interesting that this idea is connected to the phrase 'Ichigu o terasu,' from Japanese Buddhism, meaning to 'light up a corner' or 'to be a light that brightens the surroundings.' You can sense true affection more profoundly in the smile of roughly carved Buddhist

"Dragon-Tiger picture" by ▶
Takamatsu Toshitsugu.

statues made by priests such as Enku and the monk Mokujiki than in imposing Buddhist statues made of gold.

If you explain history with only a shallow understanding of Budo, Budo looses its charm and appeal. When this happens, it is important to listen to the drumbeats and marches that accompanied the Meiji Restoration— listen to the rhythm of change, which we can liken to the revival of Budo. I urge you to listen to the hidden bufu while following the path of 'learning from the past.' In Budo, if you are always chasing after the new you will loose sight of its important secrets. This revival of Budo, or restoration of imperial rule (ouseifukko, 王政復古) can be equated with the concept of 'to die and come back to life' (ouseifukko, 往生復呼). What I am trying to say is we should always immerse ourselves in sunlight, and in Budo training, never forget to smile, and never be surprised regardless of what happens.

Budo and the arts

The vitality of the Bushi is demonstrated in the craftsmanship of their armor and weapons, and it is said that the tearooms of the Kinkakuji

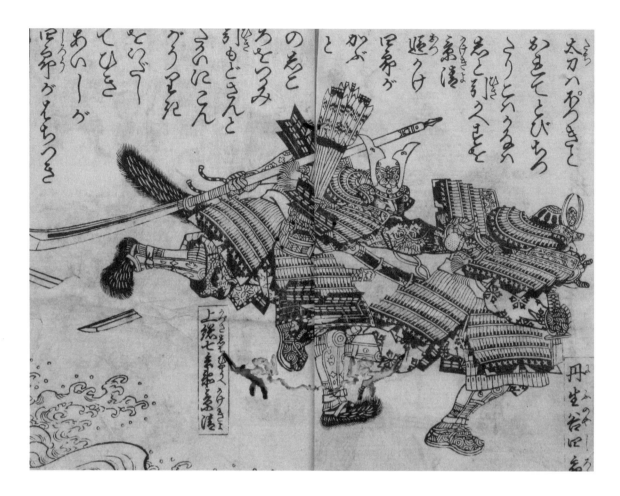

and Ginkakuji were made in order to display their power. It is possible, however, they might have been created solely to display the aesthetic sense of powerful people.

With the advent of the gun, the utility of the sword diminished, and this was damaging for followers of Bushido. The flame of Bushido burned out in the Warring States period. At that time, if the samurai had already known the common value of things globally, like diamonds, their fate might have been considerably different. The diamond or ruby inlaid into the brow of a statue of Buddha, the so-called third eye, may indicate the consciousness of that Buddha statue. Oda Nobunaga and Toyotomi Hideyoshi awarded their military leaders with the swords of well-known makers, or the works of fine potters, in place of thousands and tens of thousands of koku of rice. In the tea ceremony, the teacup was considered highly precious, and Nobunaga and Hideyoshi would also give these as gifts. I hear the Dutch painter Helene Muller said that art is the human form made into the soul. If this is the case, how should we see the soul of the warrior and the spirit of Japan? Perhaps by looking at the form of a martial artist well trained in the martial traditions we can perceive the meaning. By so doing, we may come to see the existence of the martial artist in both ourselves and others.

The illusionist Japanese painter Hayami Gyoshu said, "In my lifetime I will continue to destroy the form," and he devoted his life to the expression of destruction; that was the essence of his art. Although the expression of destruction may change, as in the painting style of Mondrian, or in Zen style paintings, all art is naturally changing, and when time passes, the works gain importance. Like coexisting with a simple, melancholic and rustic feeling (the Japanese concept of wabi and sabi), so the ability to change naturally is a power also shared by the sword saint, and it helps protect them from enemies.

What is the gokui?

My belief is that the gokui, or essence, is living with change (henka). If people change then things change and the times change. It would be strange, therefore, if each respective era didn't have gokui. Ironically, gokui is about change; people and times must change, but the fundamental aspect of gokui does not change. Budo has existed for thousands of years and the fact that my Budo is understood around the world shows that it exists within something that is like the gokui.

Therefore, even if you don't understand the gokui, it is best to tie yourself to a good friend and teacher and persevere with bufu ikkan. 'Gokui' can be read as the numbers 5-9-5 (go-ku-i, 五九五) in Japanese. If we contemplate this, we find that five is the supreme number for the age of the gods and nine means the present, it gives rise to experiences. You can see the gokui in the henka (change) of these numbers.

In a somewhat paradoxical sense, when you think the gokui exists, it does not, but if you think it doesn't, it appears in the scrolls of the dead like a miracle. The existence of the gokui is truly mysterious. It is a fact that people possess caliber. Didn't the Rakugo master Yanagiya Kosan (1915–2002) say it as well? It is important to learn, but some people cannot progress even if they try hard at learning—they don't have the capacity. This is why some kabuki actors don't teach to their successors or students. Nevertheless, there are very talented people that come forth

to inherit the traditional arts. There is luck in great achievement in Budo. This is why so many people jump to the conclusion that someone who says "the way of the samurai is not found in death," actually fears death. However, the law of the warrior is to be patient until the end. It is important to understand that dying in anger is a waste. If you look at the death of many talented artists such as Van Gogh and Mozart, it is natural to feel pity for them. It is my wish that you to listen to the divine tune of the didactic poem—"Water is sure to fall to the ground, but the time it falls is that of the beginning of its ascent." In that way, the spirit of the Bushi that transcends the natural stages of birth, aging, sickness, and death is passed on to future generations.

I was instructed in the bufu by a master teacher and because of this saw the heaven of countless pleasures within transcendence. Rushing to one's death because you are not recognized by the world is to fault the will of the gods. This is truly a sad moment for those that possess great talent. Life force can be nurtured and cultivated; however, there is something that transcends even this. When I was once making an offering to the kamidana (household altar), somehow the nearby candles reflected light in the form of a cross (jumonji, 十文字) on to the kamidana. I thought this was strange, and when I told this to my teacher, he said, "Ah, you are bound to something in the universe." I urge you to feel the importance of these insights from nature. For me, each word my teacher uttered helped me to progress. This is a natural thing, but I think it is good if you can do these things yourself. Furthermore, motivation is important. And in this you can see the magnetic power of the gokui that attracts master and student. I have recently been feeling strongly that to make someone do something beyond their capacity is going against the will of the gods. In order to be connected to the gods, one must live within the same flow as one's teacher and the gods.

Calligraphy by Kon Toko.

Transcending common sense

As when looking at fine swords, it is unwise to make hasty judgements when viewing literature. Just like there are times when sudden light can damage the eyes, reacting to things in an instant can be dangerous. Fortune telling has recently enjoyed some popularity, however, to draw conclusions is the beginning of failure.

To leave things ambiguous and not judge the truth of matters that are uncertain, aesthetically speaking, is connected to the world of the subtle and profound (yugen no sekai). Even if you envelop things in smoke, there are many types of smoke. There is the smoke of pollution, the smoke of the benevolent Emperor, and the smoke of the Ninja.

A Budo researcher once said to me, "I researched many different schools of martial arts and published books, but it never amounted to anything." I replied, "Isn't it fine to know that it didn't amount to anything? It is because of the expression 'all things are one.'" Actually, the same thing can be said about bugei (martial arts). It is crucial to know that to research something will amount to nothing. Speaking of the oneness of things, the number one has a plus one (+1) and minus one (−1), with the zero as the balance point. If you understand the principle of one very deeply then the cosmic dual forces of In and Yo philosophy will become clear.

Budo is the direction to live and the readiness to know consciousness (shiki, 識). Consciousness also takes the form of the four seasons (shiki, 四季), commands (shiki, 指揮), palpitations of death (shiki, 死悸), morale of the troops (shiki, 士気), rhythm of poetry (shiki, 詩悸) and the capacity of man (shiki, 士器). If you try to rely on the common opinion of history and books, then you will not be able to see the reality of history.

Furthermore, in history, many varying opinions and eccentric views are mixed together, and new theories frequently emerge. Therefore, it becomes very difficult to distinguish truth from falsehood. In this book I seek to express the importance of abandoning this kind of general common sense and opinion for a moment, and instead looking at the true form of things. Nonetheless, if one does not have real training, then doing this will amount to nothing.

Kon Toko (1898–1977), the charismatic author, chief abbot of the Hiraizumi Chuson temple, and a one-time member of the National Diet of Japan, wrote the words: "pure heart is the training hall" (magokoro kore dojo). These words are indeed true; it is magokoro that enables transcendence from good and evil, life and death, victory and defeat, good fortune and bad fortune. This wise saying relates to the gokui of Budo.

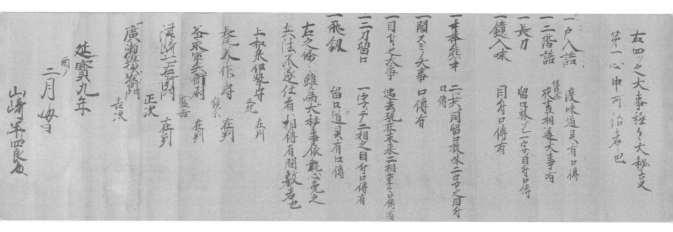

The Direction of Bushi

It is said that the martial ways are shown through one's daily life and behavior. Namely, through the manners of humanity. Needless to say, the Budoka who avoids thoughtless or inappropriate behavior is not consumed by rashness; he maintains a calm attitude, does not hesitate, but is modest, full of kindness, and is highly respected. The true path of the martial ways is to not let one's eagerness take control. Although it is said to be honorable is to protect the weak and fight the strong, it is not permitted to fight unnecessarily or without reason. When the circumstances necessitate, however, those who do not fear the strong and protect the weak should be called true warriors. When someone insults or disrespects you, the courage to laugh and not make them an opponent is true courage. Taking up the sword unnecessarily should be avoided at all costs. Maintaining a graceful heart together with the virtue of affection that is genial and pleasant, while also retaining the stern temperament to be decisive and bold; valuing both the literary and military arts without being carried away by learning; possessing a well balanced heart of kindness and valor: this is the divine warrior. We should persevere in this eternal direction of the warrior.

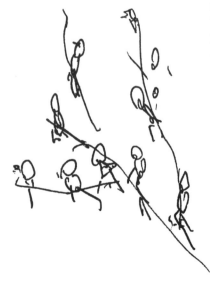

武士の心得として起居動作則ち礼儀
を慎み人道を過たざるを武威と言ひ相應尾籠の振る舞ひをやうに又程宜に
流れず悠揚迫らず厳然腹せず慎み深く慈愛に富み厳も武勇を尊重
するは申す迄も無く気に怒りと雖も血気に任せ乱暴狼籍にならぬ様要武風
の深く戒める所也弱者を挫け強者と雖も猥りに
弱者を挫くと雖も難も猥りに争う事は許さず止むを得ぬ場合
に争う事は許さず止むを得ぬ場合弱者を挫けこと
強きをも怒れず弱者を挫けこと恥辱と興
真の武人と云う可きぞ
える者あよども笑う相手せる可力
がと奥の帝也同時に猥りに刀に手を
かける事絶対に慎む可し則ち
則ち秘翻烈日のぬき勇気果断の

気象に伴ぶに春風駘蕩たる慈愛
の徳と共に優雅なる心を保持し
文武を貴び文弱に流るる事無く
一方的に片よらず武勇と共に優しき
心を知るを真の武神と人が云う
これ武人の常の心得と誓うべし
武徳八幡神万変不驚日々常に
花情和を以て莞爾として微笑む
これ八活秘剣の武徳を会得する
ための心構なり

平成十七年三月十日

初見良昭
白龍翁

Rei 礼

In the daily practice of Budo, etiquette begins with a bow. The etiquette of Budo is contained within the five Confucian virtues of benevolence, justice, etiquette, wisdom, and sincerity. Etiquette is the cornerstone of these values, and it is important to realize this balance. Fully understanding this means you will never stray from the natural path of bushido.

Snow, Moon, and Flower　雪月花

Snow, Moon, and Flower　雪月花

Kumidachi　組太刀

Kumidachi is cultivating the unification of unarmed fighting, and fighting with weapons such as the tachi and long weapons. This means always having the driving force of taijutsu present; thus miraculous taijutsu and tachi become the life force and reveal the true form of 'hiken.'

In speaking of kuraidori (positioning), there is positioning in kamae as well. Depending on the warrior's position, their humanity, in other words, the splendor and terror will naturally reveal itself. This is not something that comes from form.

Seigan no Kamae　正眼の構　　　　　Chudan no Kamae　中段の構

Seigan no Kamae 正願の構

Seigan no Kamae 青眼の構

Fudo no Kamae　不動の構

Tenchi Hasso no Kamae　天地八相の構

Hiryu no Kamae　飛龍の構

Chosui no Kamae 澄水の構

Kasumigakure no Kamae　霞隠の構

Muso no Kamae　夢想の構

Uranami no Kamae
浦波の構

Roppo Kuji no Kamae
六方九字の構

Dato no Kamae
打柝の構

天覆神元神妙神通力

天靈神元神気神道力

天靈神元神気神道力

Muto Dori Hiden 無刀（武闘）捕り秘伝

Many people think that Muto dori is about the opponent wielding a sword while you have none, but this is not the case. Even if you have a sword, muto dori starts with the development of the courage to face an opponent with the preparedness of not having a sword. This means if you don't thoroughly train in taijutsu you will not obtain the knowledge of the refined skill of Muto dori. Therefore, you must first know the purpose of the path of training. If you are unaware of this and proceed down the path of thinking that sword training is only about cutting and thrusting, then there is a danger that you will go down the path of the evil sword. The sword harnesses a pure essence that is life-giving—one who cannot live the way of the sword saint will foolishly think that the sword is only a tool for cutting. Those who do this can never achieve enlightenment.

The warrior's heart is ruled by preparedness, and nature's heart, or god's heart, is fundamental. The heart also governs the warrior's physical kamae. Therefore, if there is no unity in spirit and body, you will never understand the reason for being a martial artist. You will leave no vulnerability or opening (suki) if you remain consistently prepared. When the opponent assumes a kamae to try and cut they will be unable to touch you. To show

the determination (kihaku) that you will immediately knock over an opponent with your fighting spirit (kiai)—this is the form of calm courage and the quiet heart of a divine posture. The enemy's attack is stayed by your determintation and they are temporarily paralyzed (fudo kanashibari) as they are knocked down from a distance by your thundering cry (to-ate no jutsu). You should know that unless you have this determination in your training then the gokui of muto dori cannot be obtained.

Here I would like to mention muto dori training as well as shinken gata (real fighting). Many people do not fully understand muto dori, and believe it is simply the knowledge of defending against a sword attack, but I would urge you to understand that it is the mind and skill of disarming the opponent, whether they wield a yari, naginata, bow, shuriken, or gun. You must understand the mind of "ten thousand changes, no surprises," and attain the knowledge of muto dori in response to infinite variations. Attaining knowledge of real muto dori means you will earn the protection of the gods. In Futen Goshin no Kamae, when the tiger and dragon fight, drawing ferocious storms, the wind gods will protect you, and you will see the light. On the other hand, Hanno Banetsu no Juji no Kamae resembles the power of a flood that washes away the fighting power of the opponent in an instant.

The water always runs down the natural slope of in the land, but that is just the beginning of the voyage.

Shunu 隼雄

The opponent moves to draw their daito. Like a falcon, hold the opponent's sword pommel with the left hand. The opponent takes one step back to draw his sword. Immediately thrust under the opponent's nose with the right thumb. The opponent is startled by this and moves back. Immediately grab the pommel of the opponent's sword with your right hand and step back drawing the opponent's sword, holding the sword blade with your left hand. Stand ready to thrust. Maintain zanshin.

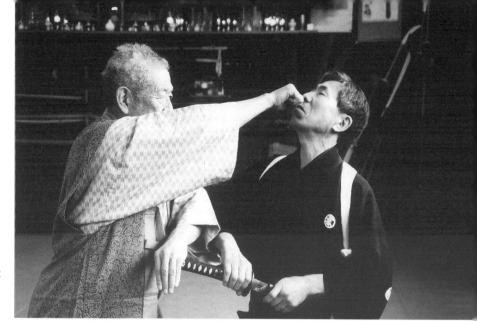

Hayato uchi. The thrust is not just with the tip of the sword, but the entire length of the sword, pommel, and the guard.

Shunsoku 隼足

The opponent moves to draw his daito. As before, control the pommel of the sword. The opponent strikes your left wrist with his right hand. Immediately rotate to the opponent's left side; with the right hand take the opponent's scabbard at the end and with the left hand take the opponent's left wrist. Lifting the right hand, control the opponent's left hand with the scabbard. The sword pommel surrounds the opponent's left leg. The opponent falls face down, and controlled by the sword. Immediately kick in with the right foot to the opponent and hold him down.

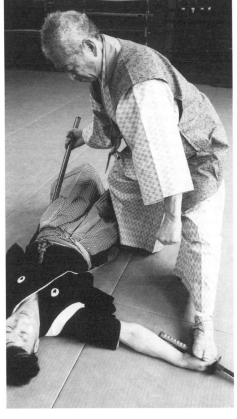

Ichigeki　一撃

The opponent is in Daijodan no Kamae (sttacking position with sword raised above the head). Immediately step in and, while controlling the opponent's left elbow, strike into the chest area of the opponent with the thumb. Kicking up with the right leg, knock the opponent onto their back. Immediately kick the side of the opponent's right leg with your right leg. The chest area (kyobu, 胸部) of an armored soldier is called the martial area (kyobu, 境武).

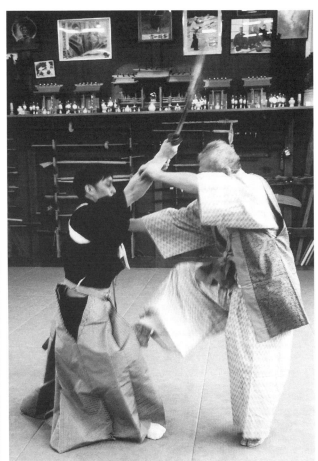

Kaisoku 魁足

The opponent cuts down from Daijodan. Shift your body to the left, avoiding the opponent's cut, which comes down along the right side of the body, and the sword flies out of the opponent's hand. Immediately kick up with your right leg to the opponent's right hand. The opponent puts his hand on the kodachi. Strike the opponent's kasumi with shuto. The opponent falls forward. Immediately take the opponent's elbow joint of the right arm with your left hand. Flip the opponent up with right osoto-gari (drawing the opponent's right foot out). Maintain zanshin.

Koryaku 拘掠

The opponent cuts in from Daijodan. Shifting onto the right foot, avoid the cut that goes past on the left side. Immediately catch the opponent's right wrist with the left hand. At the same time grab the opponent's right elbow with the right hand, and together with both legs let the opponent flow past the right side as they fall forward. This becomes a sutemi; immediately rise and maintain zanshin.

This movement is the same with our without a sword.

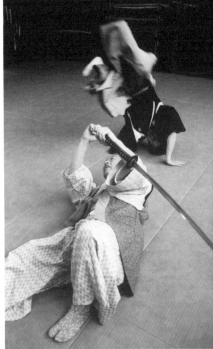

Iaifuji 意合封

The opponent cuts in horizontally from the right side. Jump back one step. The opponent moves into Daijodan. Immediately jump in with the left arm up to receive the arms of the opponent and strike the opponent's left chest with the thumb of the right hand. Immediately kick the opponent over with the right leg, then retreat and maintain zanshin. The right thumb can be replaced by a dagger or a spear, etc.

Chingan 沈雁

The opponent stands in Seigan. You are in Banetsu no Kamae. The opponent immediately thrusts in. Immediately sink the body and turn to the left; the opponent's cut flows by the right side. With the left hand, strike and take the opponent's right wrist. Immediately placing the right hand, sink the body. With the hand holding the opponent's sword, turn the sword to the left overhead, pulling the left leg back, and sit. Kicking with the right leg, the opponent falls forward. Maintain zanshin. This kick is both a physical attack and a strike to the spirit.

Fuu 風盃

The opponent cuts in from Daijodan. Turn the body to the left and control the opponent's sword blade in front of the tsuba with the right hand by laying the fingers over the top of the tsuba. Immediately strike with a left shuto (hand sword) directly into the face of the opponent and pull the sword from the opponent's grip. This is also called "taking the real sword" (shinken tori). Holding the sword with the left hand, cut to the side of the opponent, knocking him over.

Mutodori; Iai dori do-gaeshi　無刀捕り・意合捕り胴返し

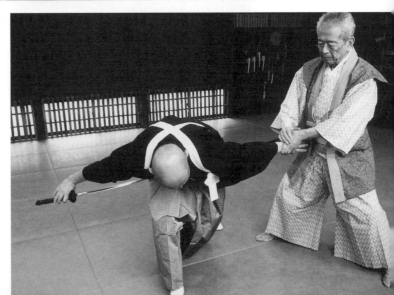

Knife hidden in a sword handle　柄隠れの一刀

There is a small knife (tanto) hidden in the handle of the sword. This can be thrown or used to thrust. This quickly changes into the juppo sessho of taijutsu. A finger can also be used to thrust.

CHAPTER 2

The Essence of Japanese Swordsmanship

The Principle of 'Pushing and Cutting' with the Sword

In ancient times there were no weapons. Although the sword and bow have existed since long ago, it appears that only chieftains and other tribal leaders bore such items. Old books record that around 500 BC, when invaders from overseas landed in Japan, attacks were repelled using primitive warfare techniques, like hand-to-hand fighting, sticks, stones, digging of defensive trenches, and to some extent the bow. Later, weapons similar to those brought from other countries were made and developed. Over time the use of weapons progressed and it is said that in the Tokugawa period (from 1603 onward) there were 120 techniques for using weapons, and from the Kan'ei period (1624) to the end of the Tokugawa military government (1867) over 3,000 martial schools emerged. The sword was born from the stick-sword of ancient times. It developed into the tachi (heavily curved sword), and later evolved into the katana (single-edged sword). In the Warring States period the musket was introduced

Picture of Yamamoto Kansuke, swordsman and military commander.

to Tanegashima island from Portugal and quickly spread across Japan. Although the power of these new weapons was widely recognized to exceed that of the sword, bow, and spear, the musket never replaced the sword in rank and importance. This was because the purpose of the sword went far beyond its function as a weapon.

The sword harnessed the authority of the ruling class and was a

Iga-Ueno Castle. ▶

symbol for the protection of spiritual peace and enlightenment. Although it was primarily a weapon, its associations were never barbaric or violent. This two-sided, or double life, of the sword is its most important feature.

Conventional wisdom holds that in education it is proper to classify swords and explain their development in the context of the history of early bamboo and wooden swords, and early tachi and katana. However, martial artists do not think like this. It is taught that the foundation of Budo is to first understand taijutsu, through which you can fight even if you have no weapons. This means to persevere in the martial ways (bufu-ikkan), and to train consistently and with utmost effort. Then you will grasp the secrets of muto dori (no-sword technique). Succeeding in this, the mysteries of the secret sword (hiken) will be revealed, and no matter what weapon you hold, your heart and your taijutsu will dance skillfully in the void (koku). Then you will be able to explain the meaning of wooden swords and bamboo swords (shinai).

At this point let us consider a tale of bamboo swords. There was once a left-handed expert called Oishi Susumu who used a 5-shaku shinai. He visited many famous dojos in Edo (now Tokyo), and fought matches with many opponents from other schools that used shorter swords. His skills would allow him to defeat one after another. After this, it is said that at the Kobuso (school for teaching vassals/retainers to the shogun), the length of shinai was fixed at 3 shaku 8 sun. Later in the Meiji period, when school kendo tournaments were still fought without fixed length shinai, those with longer shinai had a higher chance of winning, so the length of the shinai was standardized. In olden times other accounts relate that in spear fighting contests, the longer weapon was stronger.

These kinds of simple stories of fencing matches, which are encounters with the unknown, also become a means (kuden) to understand the balance between real fighting and competition.

Kendo, a sport that uses shinai or bokken following the prohibition of swords in 1912, is different from a real fight, which is decided with a

"Summer grass
All that remains
Of the warrior's dreams."

'sudden thrust or cut to the body.' In a real sword fight the technique of 'pushing and cutting' (oshikiri) is used. The world of real fighting surpasses that of form (kata). When the opponent cuts in with his sword, you pull your own sword back, his body and sword enter in, and you knock him down by pushing. In combat you can see some people continue to cut in reflexively without realizing that they have been cut by the sword of the opponent. Knowing the technique of oshikiri reduces the degree of danger.

As the great master of Buddhism and calligraphy Kobo Daishi showed by not selecting a particular brush, the reason warriors do not choose between the shinai, bokken, or katana is because they understand muto dori. Facing an opponent, armed with a sword, adapting to change (henka), hiding in the void (koku), accepting change, and acquiescing to the void—this is never about killing the opponent or benefiting from the aggression of your allies. The true meaning of Myofuken (miraculous sword) and Shinken shiraha tori (seizing a real, drawn sword) are revealed in the light and shadow as if flash frames in a movie.

The Aesthetics of Arms and Armor, or the Beautification of the Soul

On the battlefield, samurai wore armor and helmets that in total had a weight of around 40kg. The taijutsu employed when wearing this armor was therefore different from the way of moving the body in modern Judo. The skill is to move in a way that you do not feel the weight. Of course, the equipment of modern soldiers is also very heavy, much more than 40kg, so the taijutsu and taihenjutsu employed by the old samurai while wearing armor is still needed today.

In a situation in which one has to fight a soldier who is protected by armor, inflicting damage with a single stroke of the sword is a very difficult technique that requires exceptional ability. This gives rise to the need for taijutsu using grappling and striking with the sword, from the first cut with the sword to thrusting and cutting into a weak area or an opening in the armor with the second cut to finishing with the third cut. It is also important to thrust and strike with the first cut. Move into kumi-uchi, strike and cut with the tachi, knock the opponent over, and take the head. The principle is the same whether you use a yari or naginata.

The outcome of a fight between warriors was decided by the severity of their wounds. Someone who had been wounded seriously would be encouraged by saying "it's only a light wound," and someone who had been wounded lightly would be encouraged by saying "it's only a scratch." One must look beyond the wound to win the fight.

Military commanders wore body armor and helmets that were designed also to be aesthetically pleasing as well as functional. Throughout history humans have been decorating their faces and bodies to improve or enhance their natural appearance. Humans do not just apply makeup to their faces, however, but also to their hearts. The clothes they wear and the weapons they carry are also a form of makeup. In other words, the world of beauty is a world of illusion or false beauty. These days, the word 'lie' (uso or kyo) is popular, and within makeup is hidden a strategy for interchanging beauty and ugliness.

Truth and lies, while opposite, are also dependent on one another. There are times when the practice of lying is used in order to sustain life. In music and in drama, although you might start with facts, in order to make a better performance, you might 'improve' the story by including untruthful things. Or you may produce something that avoids the dangers of the times and, although not completely truthful, still speaks to people's hearts. This is because the truth that is hidden in a lie can reach the heart that is hidden deep within a person. This is one example of heart-to-heart communion without words. Observing a scene from

Statue of Miyamoto Musashi.

the drama *The Kanjincho Scroll of Kanadehon Chushingura: The Treasury of Loyal Retainers* would illustrate this point effectively. It is said that the body of Miyamoto Musashi, based on his wishes, is buried standing in full armor. This has added to the poetic notion that he wanted to live on as a warrior beyond his death.

The Connection Between the Sword and Spear

It is said that techniques of the spear (sojutsu) were created in the Warring States period. During these times, the spear was advantageous in order to thrust into an opening, knock down, or cut down a warrior protected by armor. Having understood this, when one sees the image of a warrior fighting with the "eight secret swords as one" (happo biken ichinyo; referring to the interchangeability of weapons), the way of the sword is revealed for the first time. Let us continue down the path of the sword and spear a little further.

Mankind first discovered digging earth and hunting animals by attaching a pointed object to the end of a long stick and spearing them. We could indeed call early humans "primitive spearmen." There are many theories on the development and history of the spear, but it is said that it was really in the Warring States period that the spear was most used, and techniques of the spear developed. The schools whose techniques I inherited taught spear techniques as secret techniques in olden times. The following record provides an example. Around 550BC, followers of Buddhism and Vedism began living in Isoshiki, and by the time of Soga no Iruka (a Buddhist ruler around 640 A.D.), the number of Vedists had increased to more than 20,000. Though Iruka ruled the area, the Vedists' power was considerable, a fact that made unification of Japan difficult, and consequently the gods became anxious. In order to address the divided nation, the gods gathered together to prepare nine laws of weaponry to protect

Densho of Muso Itto-ryu.

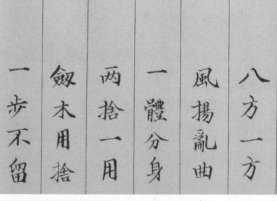

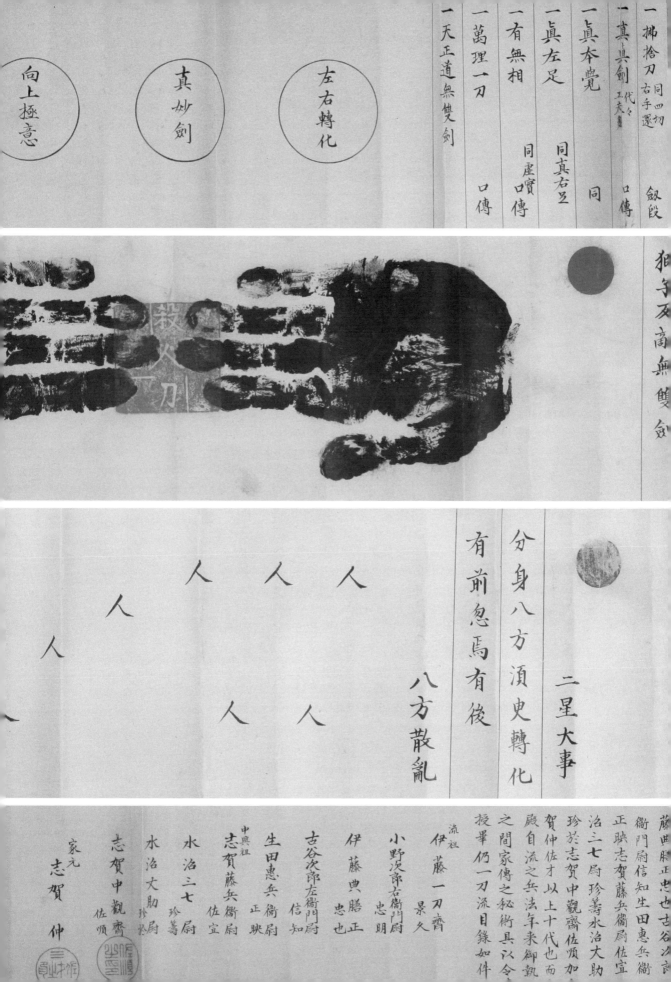

一拂捨刀　古手還　同四切

一眞具劍　代々工夫真　飯段

一眞本覺　口傳　同

一眞左足　同眞右足

一有無相　同虛實　口傳

一萬理一刀　口傳

一天正道無雙劍

◯ 向上極意　◯ 真妙劍　◯ 左右轉化

猶予及尚無雙劍

殺人刀

二星大事

分身八方須史轉化

有前忽焉有後　八方散亂

人　人　人　人　人　人　人

藤田勝正忠也古谷次郎
衛門尉信知生田惠兵衛
正映志賀藤兵衛尉佐宜
治三七局珍籌水治大助
珍於志賀中觀齋佐順加
賀仲佐才以上十代也而
殿自流之兵法年来御凱
之間家傳之秘衛其以令
授畢仍一刀流目錄如件

流祖　伊藤一刀齋　景久

小野次郎右衛門尉　忠明

伊藤典膳正　忠也

古谷次郎左衛門尉　信知

中興祖　生田惠兵衛尉　正映

志賀藤兵衛尉　佐宜

水治三七局　珍籌

水治大助　珍於

志賀中觀齋　佐順

家元　志賀仲

Japan from the Vedists and Buddhists. The methods they outlined were known as 'kyuho,' which means the way of the nine weapons:

1. Castle construction—stone walls and stone houses.

2. Stone cross—stone of six corners in a cross.

3. Bow—eagle-feather arrows made of peach tree wood. A bow of three shaku.

4. Sword—attaching a stone sword to the end of Shogun Tree wood (mukunoki).

5. Spear—attaching a stone tip to the end of six shaku of Shogun Tree wood.

6. Bo staff—eight shaku of Shogun Tree wood.

7. Halberd arrow—attaching a spear-like object that cuts on both edges to three shaku of Shogun Tree wood.

8. Halberd—a spear that cuts on both edges.

9. Tenmon, Chimon—horse-back tactics, etc.

Later, during the first year of the period of Engen (1336–40), and from this time, the sword, spear, and other weapons took on their modern forms. There are many writings that are extremely useful to discover the principles of using the spear. The reason that the spear became so important in the Warring States period was that it was far easier to strike into the gaps in the armor of an opponent by stabbing in and knocking them down, than to try and cut an opponent with a tachi. The swordsmen who have been revered as masters by later generations used the most practical and effective weapons on the battlefield. Iizasa Ienao was a master of the naginata, Iizasa Morinobu was an expert in Shinto-ryu spear techniques, and Tsukahara Bokuden was a master of the bow and spear. Bokuden later initiated Honma Kageyuzaemon in spear fighting. Koizumi Isenokami, praised as the best spearman of Kozuke country, was both a master swordsman and master of the spear.

Let us introduce a section of the densho I received that has a record regarding spear techniques. A look at this gives us an idea of the process by which a master spearmen is born, starting with a basis in taijutsu and subsequently developing spear skills. Looking at the densho of Shinden Fudo-ryu Daken-taijutsu, the school was founded by Izumo Yoshiteru in the Eikyu period (1113–18), and Shinmon Yoshikane developed it in taijutsu, sword technique, and spear technique in the Shocho period (1428–29). Mizuhara Yoshinari, the lord who, according to legend, was the illegitimate child of Minamoto no Yoshitsune, was said to be not only a master of taijutsu, horsemanship, sword technique, and spear technique but also the master of iai in the seventh year of the Kencho period (1256).

Picture of Minamoto no ▶
Yoshiie, military commander.

八幡太郎
源義家

八幡太郎義家八
六孫王経基乃
末葉めそ
頼義の
長子あり
源氏正続めて
奥州後三年の
戦ひみ高名と
なりつかふ

Picture of a Tessen.

There were many schools of the spear, and a great variety of types and lengths of spears. There were those that were less than 5 shaku, those over 2 ken, and those over 1 jo. All spears were basically categorized as hand spears (te yari) and long bladed spears (taishin yari). The handles of spears were made with various types of wood including red and white oak and from the locquat tree. There were also spear handles made by applying split and lacquered bamboo strips. Furthermore, there were also the iron spears (tetsu yari) made with iron handles, and so-called kama yari (the tip of which was shaped like a sickle), three-pronged spears (sanbon yari), tube spears (kuda yari), hook spears (kagi yari), and there was a cross-shaped spear (jumonji yari). Spears are classified by their shape and the way of attaching the blade to the handle. Other types included simple spears (su yari), socket spears (fukuro yari), sickled spears (kama yari), single-bladed spears (kikuchi yari), single-sickle spears (katakama yari), and long-bladed spears (taishin yari). Inevitably, the unification of the heart, body, and spear gave birth to innumerable divine techniques, and the inheritance of spear fighting (sojutsu), which became the core of the many different schools, was born.

The Meaning of Kyusho

Let us talk a little about vital points (kyusho, 急所), as generally used in martial arts. When considering kyusho, areas such as the pit of the stomach, throat, and neck are often mentioned, but when someone is wearing armor these areas are covered or protected. Depending on the school, the word 'kyusho' is sometimes written with the characters for nine places

Picture of the warrior ▶
Mihonoya Shiro.

or nine varieties. The characters kyusho (窮所), meaning 'places of suffering or perplexity,' can also be used.

In real combat, the moment you think kyusho exist, they cease to; when you think they do not exist, they do. You must know the kyojitsu of the kyusho. The knowledge of points used in moxibustion and acupuncture and the knowledge of kyusho as used in Budo are completely different. To "show a kyusho" (reveal an opening) can provoke an attack which can reveal the opponent's kyusho, and from which you can plan a counter. In this sense, it is a type of strategy (heiho).

As in the martial verse of the bo-jutsu gokui: "Thrusting the end of the bo into the void, if you feel a response; that is the gokui," there is a teaching to attain the secret of kyusho 急所 which reads "thrust the kyusho in the void." It is said that the singer Misora Hibari, when immersed in recording (which would be the equivalent of actual combat for a Budoka) always sang perfectly, which prompted one songwriter to comment, "However many times she sings she really sings perfectly in the void, like a skylark singing in the sky." To hit a kyusho, first know the truth of hicho no jutsu and tengu tobikiri no jutsu, (leaping methods), then throw your heart to the sky and hit the mark with the feeling of "all or nothing."

The Tachi and the Way of the Warrior

Since the Tensho period (1573–92) of the Warring States period, the length of the tachi was from 2 shaku 2 sun to 2 shaku 3 or 4 sun at its longest. Incidentally, although it varied depending on the time and region, the average height of a Japanese male until the early part of the Meiji period was less than 160 cm (5 shaku 3 sun). According to the Taiheiki, the tachi of Nawa Nagatoshi in the Genko period (1331–33) was 4 shaku 3 sun. Saji Magozaburo of Tanba carried a tachi of 5 shaku 3 sun. In the time of Emperor Gomurakami, Wada Masatomo's tachi was 4 shaku 5 sun, and it is said that Fujiwara no Yasunaga drew a tachi of 4 shaku 8 sun. Tsumaga Nagamune carried a tachi of 5 shaku 3 sun. In the time of the battle of the Fuefuki Pass, Yazu Kojiro had a tachi of 6 shaku 3 sun. Akamatsu Ujinori carried a tachi of 5 shaku 7 sun. The sword of Togashi Masachika appears in the tales of storytellers as 9 shaku 3 sun.

The Ninja sword had a blade length of 1 shaku 6 to 7 sun. In the Tokugawa period, a blade longer than 2 shaku was called a katana. Up to 1 shaku 9 sun was called an o-wakizashi, up to 1 shaku 7 sun was called a chu-wakizashi, and up to 9 sun 9 bu was called a sho-wakizashi. The uchi-gatana that began to appear from the Muromachi period were initially 1 shaku 4 sun, but towards the end of the period went from 1 shaku 7 or 8 sun to 2 shaku in length.

Picture of Miyamoto ▶
no Yoshiie.

With the daito and shoto (a pair of long and short swords), the long sword is sometimes made into a naginata or yari, and the long and short swords are used together as a pair. The short sword was also effective when used in confined spaces against multiple enemies. There is a proverb: "The short sword can be used as a long sword and the long sword as a short sword."

Real common sense means, when in a fight, look with 'extraordinary eyes' (kime, 奇眼). Kime are also an example of "the eyes of god" (shingan, 神眼); when in combat, this becomes kaname (神眼) (another reading of shingan), also meaning the 'key' or 'main point,' said to be a very important insight. The 'key' to the incident in which Nasu no Yoichi played a crucial role for the Genji clan in defeating the Heike clan is contained in this idea. Yoichi was a famous archer who hit the ceremonial war fan of the invading Heike fleet at sea with an impossible shot, providing a symbolic prelude to the defeat that awaited them.

When you think of using a weapon you are at once enslaved by it. It is important to consider not carrying a sword, not wielding a stick, but using what is available at the time as a weapon. Anything can become a weapon. Look at a thing's advantages and disadvantages as a weapon or at armor, shields, and horses—anything natural or manmade can be used as a weapon.

"The way of the samurai is found in death." Time passes, seasons continue to change—the four seasons, shiki 四季, phonetically share the same sounds as the timing of death, shiki 死悸; reminding us of the cyclic properties of life and death.

If you unravel the phrase "ni no tachi" (usually referring to the idea of two strikes, where the first is a setup for the second) into a first and second sword, you find the small and large swords of the daisho and the use of two swords in combination. You can also see that nito (二刀, two swords used together) can mean nito (二闘, two fights). The ni no tachi of fighting in armor is the kukan (空間) through which one enters the world of fighting; it is a method of thrusting through and entering the defences of an opponent. In the case that you and the opponent are not wearing armor, ni no tachi naturally changes. Two swords then become 'with sword' and 'without sword,' also 'serious' (shinken, 真剣) or 'real sword' (shinken, 真剣).

The sword, naginata, and yari change according to the times. In the secret scrolls of the Shinkage-ryu, *Tengusho Hiden no Maki* are the names of illustrations of techniques—Ransho, Kokyoku, Unsetsu, and Denko—and pictures of samurai using long and short swords. Someone lacking knowledge in bufu would undoubtedly recall the image of the long and short swords being used in Miyamoto Musashi's Nito-ryu. Masters like Koizumi

Isenokami would probably have derided a Bugeisha with such a limited sense: they'd have explained that in such a picture, it is essential that the figure have a tachi in one hand, and a yari, naginata, or nagamaki in the other; explaining that it was a secret meaning. Thus, the picture *Tengusho Hiden no Maki* has a secret meaning, and people who are not familiar with the period of fighting with a tachi can never truly understand. The point is that the kodachi is not just a kodachi—a yoroidoshi (dagger), a spearhead, the blade of a naginata, and unarmed combat all have the same role; they are all used for the same purpose and are interchangeable. I urge you to see this as a fight scene depicting koteki ryoda of juppo sessho.

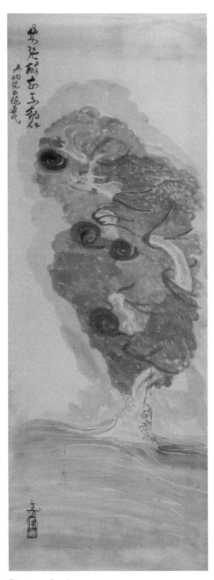

Picture of a dragon.

Picture of the priest Dharma.

Nuku 瓊躯—抜く

When drawing the sword, initiating the movement by placing the thumb on the tsuba is generally called koiguchi o kiru. However, the 'In,' or hidden, version of this technique uses the index finder and ring finger to push from below.

The forearm, elbow, and body are used to draw the sword with the left or right hand. This expression for the method of initiating the draw, koiguchi o kiru, meaning literally "cutting the carp's mouth," resembles the phrase "carp climbing a waterfall," or "ascending carp," (shori, 昇鯉) which has the same sound as the word 'shori' (勝利), meaning 'victory.' Therefore, to know the way of drawing the sword that leads to victory, it is essential to know the phenomenon of In and Yo. People who understand this phenomenon can understand the real form of Kage-ryu and can see the way of drawing the sword. This tsuba is a commemorative work made by Sanjugo Naoki, and the name of the work was carved into the tsuba.

Tenchijin no Kamae 天地人の構

The master swordsman from Akita district, Ono-oka Takatoshi, was famous for his use of Tenchijin no Kamae. The sword is held diagonally in a position close to the right ear with 9 sun (1 sun = approximately 3.03 cm) between the sword and the body. If the left leg is pulled back, then a cut can enter the opponent's left side with considerable force. For example, if the opponent's sword cuts in first, Ono-oka would immediately parry this cut and return a cut. Then, if the right leg is pulled back, a powerful cut can be initiated to the face.

Tsuki 突

Control with the tip of the sword (kissaki, 切先). This is also the tip of the spirit (kissaki, 気先). As you can see from the photograph, the opponent's kote (forearm) is covered as well as the entire body.

Kote 小手

If this is seen in a flash of inspiration; the rhyme of the thousand-armed Goddess of Mercy of the Sanjusangendo can be heard.

八面六臂

八面玲瓏

陸兵闘争者
陳列お�▲

切下げ
れる

臨兵闘者皆
陳列在布

天元輔弼證心
神通力

Goshintai; body in self defence 護身体

It is important to wear the daito and the shoto in the same manner; just as it is the same when either sword is thrust at you.

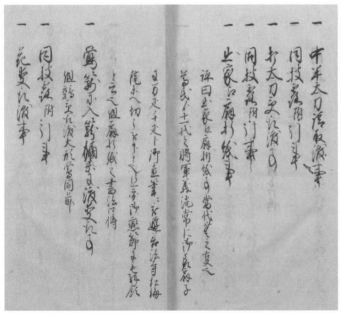

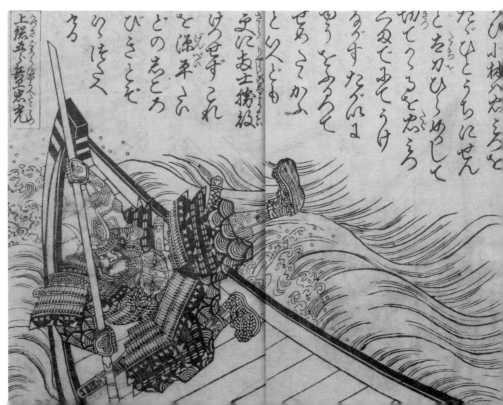

Placing the tachi in the belt, rotate behind and tie back the sleeves with the sageo.

The sword is drawn. Do not rush the draw.

Receive the handle of the opponent's sword while maintaining the character eight 八.

This becomes eight swords, while drawing changes to eight directions. Then pray and emanate ki energy.

Happo Biken 八法秘剣

- Gunryaku (war strategy) and tenmon chimon (astrology and physiography)
- Jojutsu and hanbojutsu
- Rokushaku bo and tai no kuraidori (body positioning)
- Naginata and bisento jutsu
- Kodachi and jutte jutsu
- Kisha (horseback riding) and suijutsu (swimming)
- Shuriken and senban-nage
- Sojutsu
- Biken

Bikenjutsu refers to taijutsu kenpo; adding bikenjutsu to the happo (eight principles) makes kyuho (nine principles), the generic term for the skills of the Bushi. The names kosshi-jutsu, koppo-jutsu, jutai-jutsu, daken-taijutsu, and ninpo-taijutsu were created to describe taijutsu, the "art of certain victory," and then the name biken jutsu was developed. In happo biken jutsu we call this position shachiteki seigan (diagonal posture). This is a kamae in which you can immediately cut the opponent if they attack. Pull your right foot behind by the width of your shoulders. For example, if the opponent thrusts or cuts to your abdomen, immediately turn the wrists and knock his sword away. Sasaki Kojiro's swallow cut (tsubame kiri) demonstrates this rhythm and use of kyojutsu.

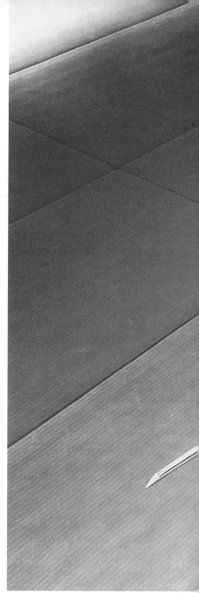

There were eight young, brave soldiers whose family names began with 犬 (dog), and they appear in a famous story entitled *Nanso Satomi Hakken-den* by Takizawa Bakin.

Tsukikomi 附込

Seigan no Kamae. The opponent is in Daijodan. Stand in Seigan pointing the sword with your whole heart (mind) at the opponent's chest; your eyes stare into the opponent's eyes. Without allowing the opponent's Daijodan to enter your thoughts, at the moment the opponent steps in to cut, let out a kiai. Just as the opponent falters, drop the left knee to the floor and thrust in.

The technique of Tsukikomi changes completely when you are wearing armor, or in the case that the opponent has a weapon or something that can be used as a shield. The place to thrust has traditionally been taught through oral transmission (kuden), since the densho is not specific of where to do so; it simply says "thrust." When thrusting in there is always variation (henka) in the thrust. At the place that you thrust, there is a lifeline (seimeisen, 生命線), or life evasion (seimeisen, 生命閃), and a death line (shisen, 死線), or death point (shisen, 死尖). Being made to remember this momentary point (sen, 尖) in combat (sen, 戦) means that by this technique, taijutsu has the power to penetrate with a dagger or thrust with a sword. Thrusting with the left foot, written with the character 'to sit,' (坐) refers to the seated posture Fudoza, the "immovable heart" (kokoro no fudo), a calm heart, a state of mind.

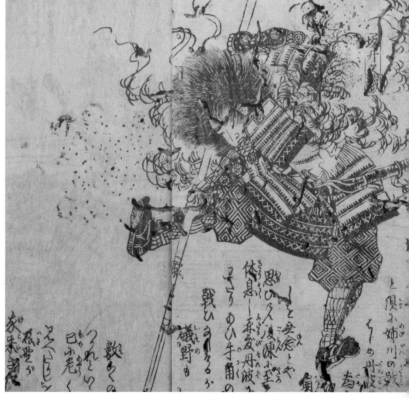

Sayugyaku (opposite position) 左右逆

Three variations. This kamae is Ichi no Kamae. Namely, the sword points straight, perpendicular to the face. If the opponent cuts in from Daijodan it is easy to flip (knock) their sword back on either the left or right. If it is flipped (knocked back) on the right, execute kote gaeshi and attack the right side of the opponent's neck. If you deflect the attack to the left, and the opponent's body turns left, perform kote gaeshi and cut the opponent completely in two.

Ichi no Kamae. First, know the principle of one (ichi) that is unity. This is the way of enlightment of Zen. Sayugyaku is not simply the opposite of left and right in a technique; the meaning is more profound and encompasses the eternal opposites of truth and falsehood, yin and yang. It is easy to think of Ichi no Kamae as a starting technique, but in fact it demands an advanced level of skill. With regard to kote, some people think that this is the area around the back of the wrists or lower arm that can be cut, but this is not the case. I would like you to think of it as small, almost imperceptible variations and techniques using the wrists as pivots. Cutting someone completely in two means within the movement, the moment you see the opening, that is the moment of opportunity—this is the secret.

Tsukigake 突掛

Seigan no Kamae. The opponent is in Daijodan. If you were to make a thrust, the opponent would cut down and both parties would be cut. Therefore, the thrust is made by stepping with the right foot then stabbing with the left foot. When doing this, if the opponent were to avoid the thrust, immediately turn the wrists and cut in to the opponent's right side.

The cultivation of taihenjutsu that tricks the opponent into thinking they have cut you makes a profound and awe-inspiring impression. Make the opponent sever the connection between cloud and water to render the opponent unable to cut you. Shine light in that space (kukan) and in that instant, turn the wrists and cut the left abdomen. If you are wearing armor, your thrust is like a shield. Turning your body, cut in (kiri-kakaru) to the opponent's right side. I would like you to think deeply about the character here—kakaru (掛). Cutting into the right side, the next move is a secret transmission. You must try to imagine the chaos of war with this idea of kiri-kakaru in mind.

Sayugyaku 左右逆

Three variations. In Gedan no Kamae, lifting the sword above the opponent's head once will confuse them. Following this deception, immediately turn the wrists and execute a right abdomen cut, or turn the hands over and execute a left abdomen cut or thrust.

In this move you strike the opponent's helmet or above their face without cutting in. However, at this time, you possess the "unmovable heart" (fudoshin), thus confusing the opponent. You make this tachi strike with your heart and the technique as one. Even though you do not cut the helmet, the force of your spirit casts down the opponent's heart—this is the spirit of kumiuchi. The small, subtle and almost imperceptible techniques of the tachi (tachi no kote) become kumiuchi; you therefore do not use dynamic techniques. Together with the body of the tachi, the handle, and the armor, cutting and thrusting into the right side and left side, you knock the opponent down and kill them.

Kiriage 斬上

Chudan no Kamae. The opponent is in Daijodan. Exactly at the instant the opponent cuts down, you turn the wrists first, and cut up from the right side to the left shoulder. At this time, if the opponent has cut down, their sword is flipped up, immediately turn the wrists and thrust in. This is called Chudan kiriage gaeshi.

There are many possible variations of your opponent's attack—he could be using no sword (muto), a kodachi, an odachi; or a sword, tachi, or katana. When your opponent cuts in, you should assume that this could be not just a single sword cut, but one with a long weapon or naginata, or a strong cut with centrifugal force. You must create the moment naturally in which you avoid or deflect the blow. This could be called the force of wind or wind power. Therefore, it is important to persevere in the martial ways (bufu ikkan; the first two characters of which are 'martial,' 武, and 'wind,' 風). In this moment, using your taijutsu technique and the power of your heart, you flip up the cut that arises from the opponent's heart, technique, and body (shingitai). At the same time, make a covering thrust at the opponent's right side, turn the wrists, and change the body and thrust up into the opponent's right side. When fighting an opponent in armor, it is advantageous to cut up.

Sayugyaku 左右逆

Three variations. Tenchijin no Kamae. Facing straight on, the sword points straight up from around the area of the right ear. The upper half of the body faces a diagonal angle to the right. The opponent cuts in from Daijodan. Pull the right foot back one step. Immediately cut up from the opponent's left side. Pull the left foot back to avoid, and cut up diagonally from the lower right.

Facing the opponent's desperate attack, this technique is executed with a kind of 'pulling through' energy (kiryoku). If you use the right foot as a pivot, cut up and chop into the opponent's left side, and if you use the left foot as a pivot, cut up into the opponent's right side. When you cut up, see in your mind your attack harmonizing with the wind power in a mountain storm blowing up from the lower side of the opponent. This then changes to 'secret sword' (biken).

Kirisage 斬下

Tenchi no Kamae. The opponent is head on. The sword is held up in front. The opponent cuts down from Daijodan. Receive the cut by drawing the left foot back; if the opponent advances, the handles of the swords meet. Push firmly, dropping the tip of the sword down to the left while turning the body to the right side, and cut down from the opponent's left shoulder. In this space (kukan) you use the fulcrum of the elbows and forearms to change and cut down with the sword.

Avoid the opponent's downward cut as though catching a ball; do not receive it head on, but adapt to its direction, alter the body position, then cut down. Giving the blade precedence (yusen, 優先), or gently avoiding the blade (yusen, 優閃), you push and cut (oshikiri), and then by changing your body position you can inflict damage on the opponent.

Sayugyaku 左右逆
Three variations. Tenchijin no Kamae. Turn the body to the left and cut up from the right side. The handles of the swords meet. Kick up and thrust in.

Kick up, according to how the opponent moves, and according to the power of the kick as it travels down. Move to attack into the opening. One technique (itte, 一手) yields endless possible variations.

Kasugaidome 鎹止 _{かすがいどめ}

Gedan no Kamae. The opponent is in Daijodan. From Gedan no kamae, move to the right and the right again (in a circle). The opponent naturally turns (corresponding to your movement). Immediately pull the left foot back, and with a kiai, raise the sword up through Chudan, Jodan no Kamae. Just after you cut down with the sword, turn right and cut the wrist over the left side of the opponent.

Rather than looking at the opponent, in kasugaidome, correct yourself by referring to the understanding of the kuden up to this point. This will bring about the destruction of the opponent's technique. The important thing here is to make your natural posture and natural heart the secret. As my master said, nature lies in a sincere spirit.

Sayugyaku 左右逆
Three variations. As before, cut up into the opponent's kote and thrust as you turn. To repeat: kote is cutting down from a close distance with a small technique.

Kochogaeshi 小蝶返

From Daijodan no Kamae. The opponent is in Seigan. Drawing your left foot back diagonally, turn swiftly to the right. Remaining in Daijodan, make a light turn to the right with the movement of a small butterfly, and at the same time cut in to the opponent's kote. This technique is also called "small butterfly cut." This is the method of the "mist butterfly" that preserves its moving strength while playing with the opponent's greater strength.

Sayugyaku 左右逆
Three variations. Turn to the right and cut at the opponent's right shoulder. Also, variations involve changing to a thrust, etc (kuden).

Shiho giri 四方斬

Tenchi Hasso no Kamae in a right diagonal posture. Reverse cut to the opponent's left side then turn the wrists. Reverse cut to the right side, then immediately enter thrusting (kuden).

Sayugyaku 左右逆
Three variations. After the last thrust, quickly cut down onto the next opponent's head. Alternatively, execute a gyaku-suso-barai.

Happo giri 八方斬

Tenchi Hasso no Kamae. This is also called a sacrifice technique (sutemi). From Hasso, cut down to the opponent's left side. Turning to the right with the body, cut down to the opponent's left side; next immediately turn to the right and cut down again in the same way.

Sayugyaku 左右逆

Three variations. This is a technique on the left, cutting the opponent in two (kuden).

Tsuki no Wa (Full Moon) 月之輪

Seigan no Kamae. From this kamae you can stab the opponent's neck by moving into Shin Ichimonji no Kamae. Also called "secret turn thrust." The character for neck (shu, 首) can also mean poem—I urge you to savor the true meaning of the Hundred Poems by the Hundred Poets.

Sayugyaku 左右逆
Three variations. Thrust into the opponent's side. Also, the technique of thrusting into the abdomen.

Kenpo of the eternal cycle of birth, death, and re-birth　生々流転その剣法

It should be taken for granted that the mental attitude of a Bushi was a secret in each school.

Yagyu-ryu Seigan no Kamae　柳生流青眼の構

The vertical Seigan no Kamae of the famous Yagyu-ryu is a special characteristic of the school.
Opening to the width of the shoulders, the tip of the sword is pointed at the opponent's eyes.
Standing in Seigan is a natural posture. There are three advantages:

1. The tip of the sword is an obstacle for the opponent, making it difficult for them to cut in.
2. If the opponent cuts in, it is possible to parry the sword behind to the left or right.
3. At the same time, it is easy to cut into the opponent's opening.

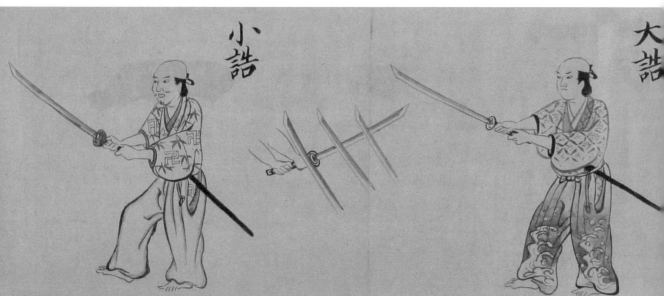

Densho of Yagyu Shinkage-ryu.

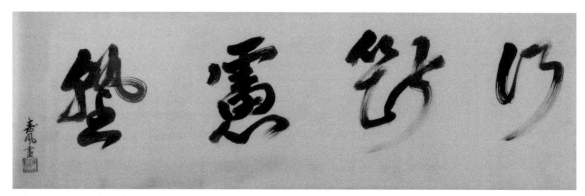

Jukuryo danko (action after contemplation.)

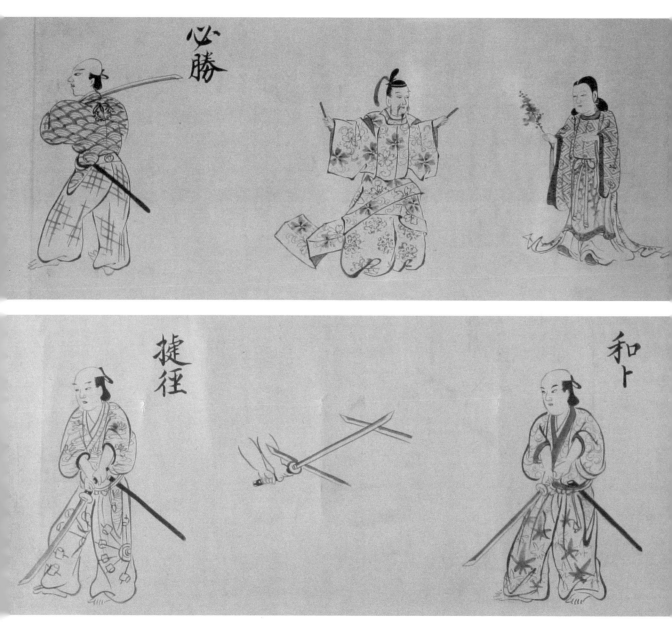

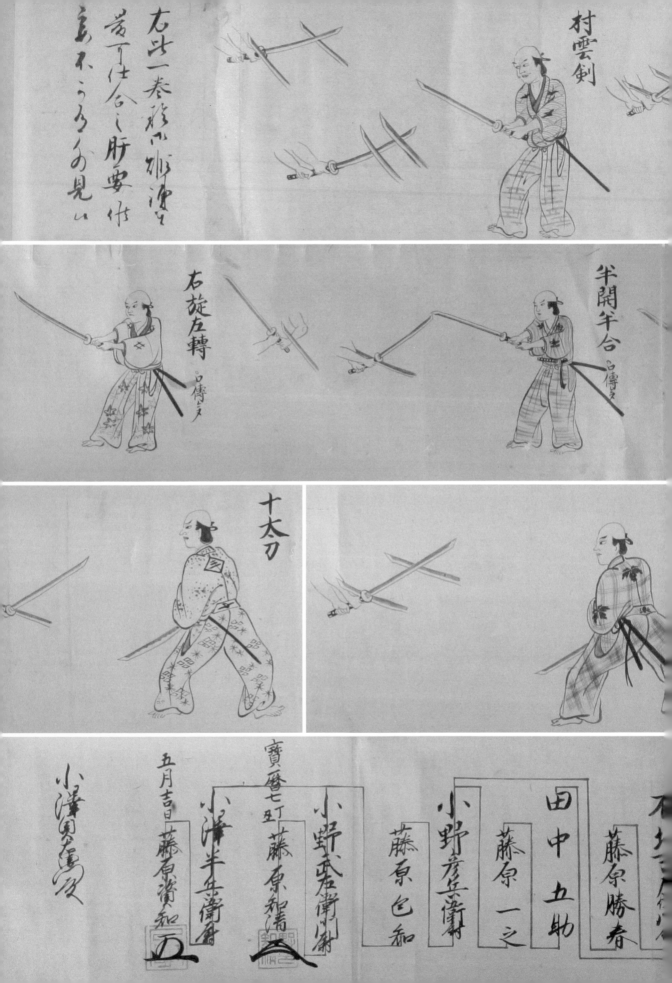

村雲剣

右此一巻於ハ……
蒡丁仕合し肝要作……
……くうタくの見ハ

右旋左轉
口傳之

半開半合
口傳之

十太刀

不知三……
藤原勝春

田中五助
藤原一之

小野彦兵衛
藤原包和

小野武左衛門

寶暦七丑
藤原知清

小澤半兵衛曆

五月吉日藤原濱和

小澤園右衛……

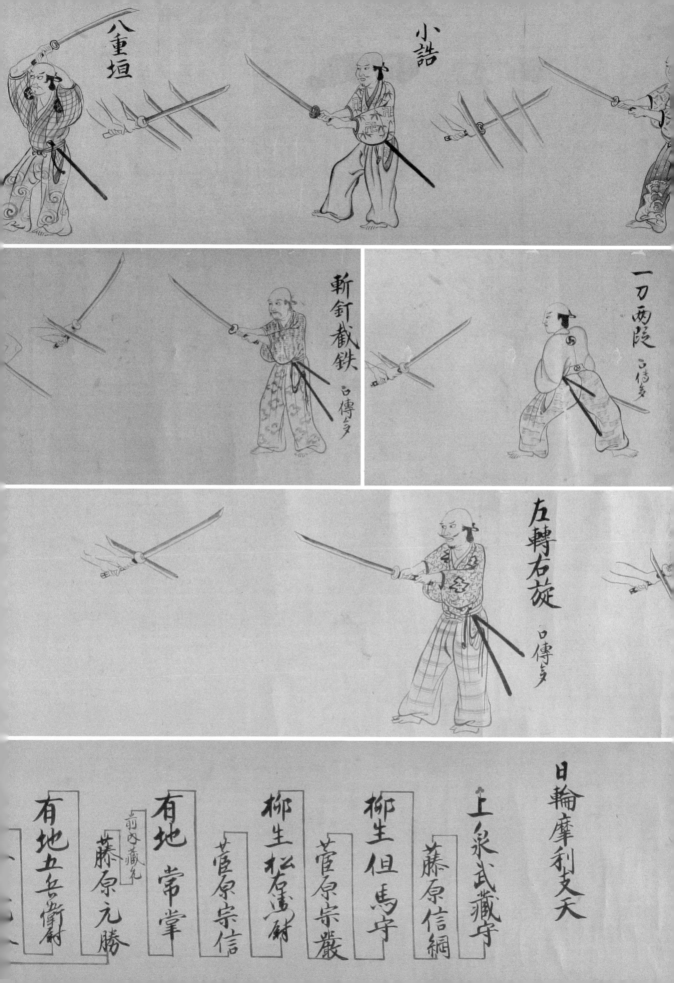

八重垣

小詰

斬釘截鉄 口傳多

一刀両段 口傳多

左轉右旋 口傳多

日輪摩利支天

上泉武藏守　藤原信綱

柳生但馬守　藤原宗嚴

柳生松右衛門　菅原宗信

有地常掌

有地　藤原元勝
前但藏元

有地五兵衛尉

氣候雑占

吾軍氣吉也

紬雨沐軍臨機莆渡

若雨煙凡燻震必勝

氣如龍如虎

武如山林

武如火烟之狀

氣候雑占終

◀ Densho on hyoho by
Koizumi Isenokami.

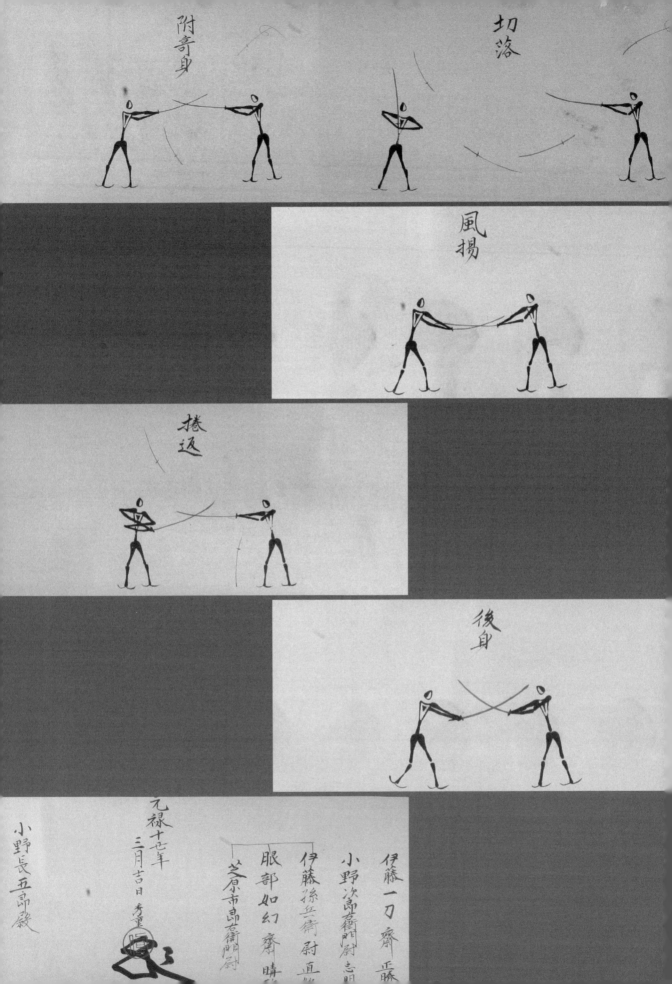

切落

附寄身

風揚

捲返

後身

小野長五郎發

元禄十四年
三月吉日　秀重

伊藤一刀齋　正藤

小野次郎右衛門尉　忠明

伊藤孫兵衛尉　直明

眼部如幻齋　晴忠

芝原市兵衛門尉

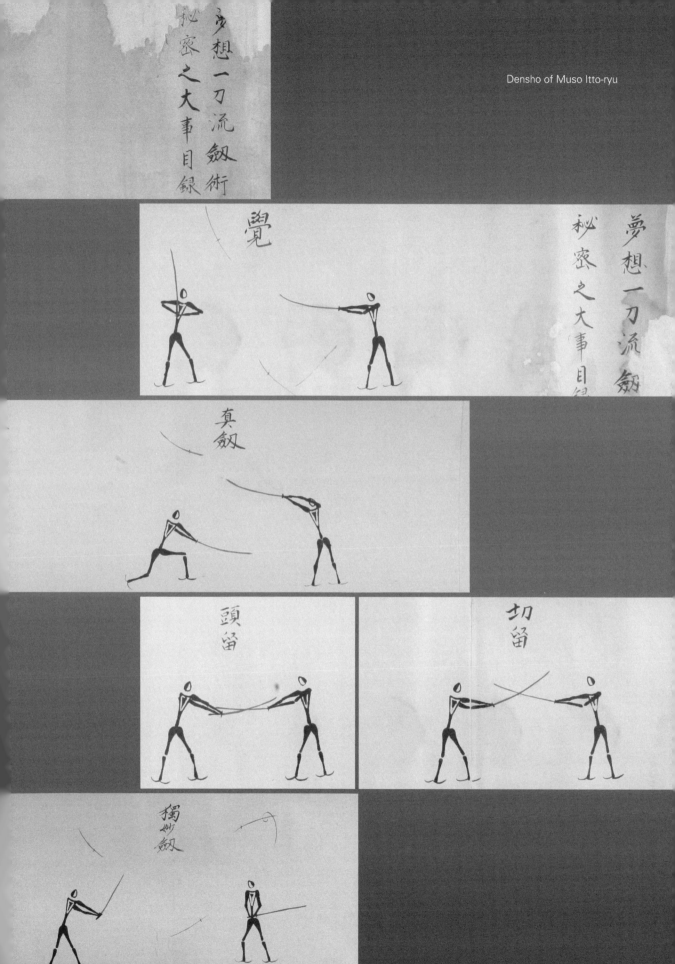

夢想一刀流劔術　秘密之大事目録

覺

真劔

頭留

切留

獨妙劔

夢想一刀流劔　秘密之大事目録

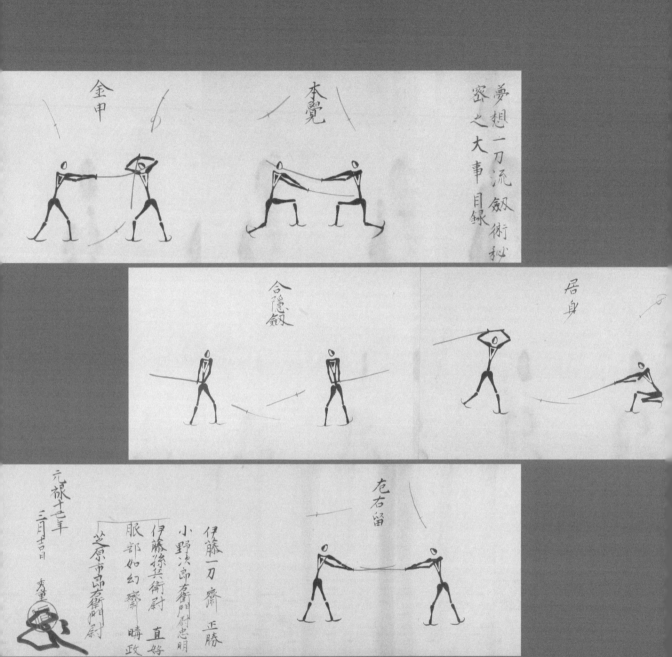

夢想一刀流劔術秘

密之大事目録

本覺

金甲

合隱劔

居身

危右留

伊藤一刀齋　正勝

小野次郎右衛門忠明

伊藤孫兵衛尉　直好

服部如幻齋　晴政

芝原市品右衛門尉

元禄十七年

三月十一日

秀重

Picture of the warrior Kato Kiyomasa killing a tiger.

Gedan no Kamae 下段の構

There was a sword master called Itori Tamenobu from the Rikuzen region. He founded the Ko-ryu and his characteristic was to stand in Gedan no Kamae. This is a posture in which he would wait for the opponent to cut in whether the opponent cuts to the side or face, hurl his sword up, and thrust into the opening.

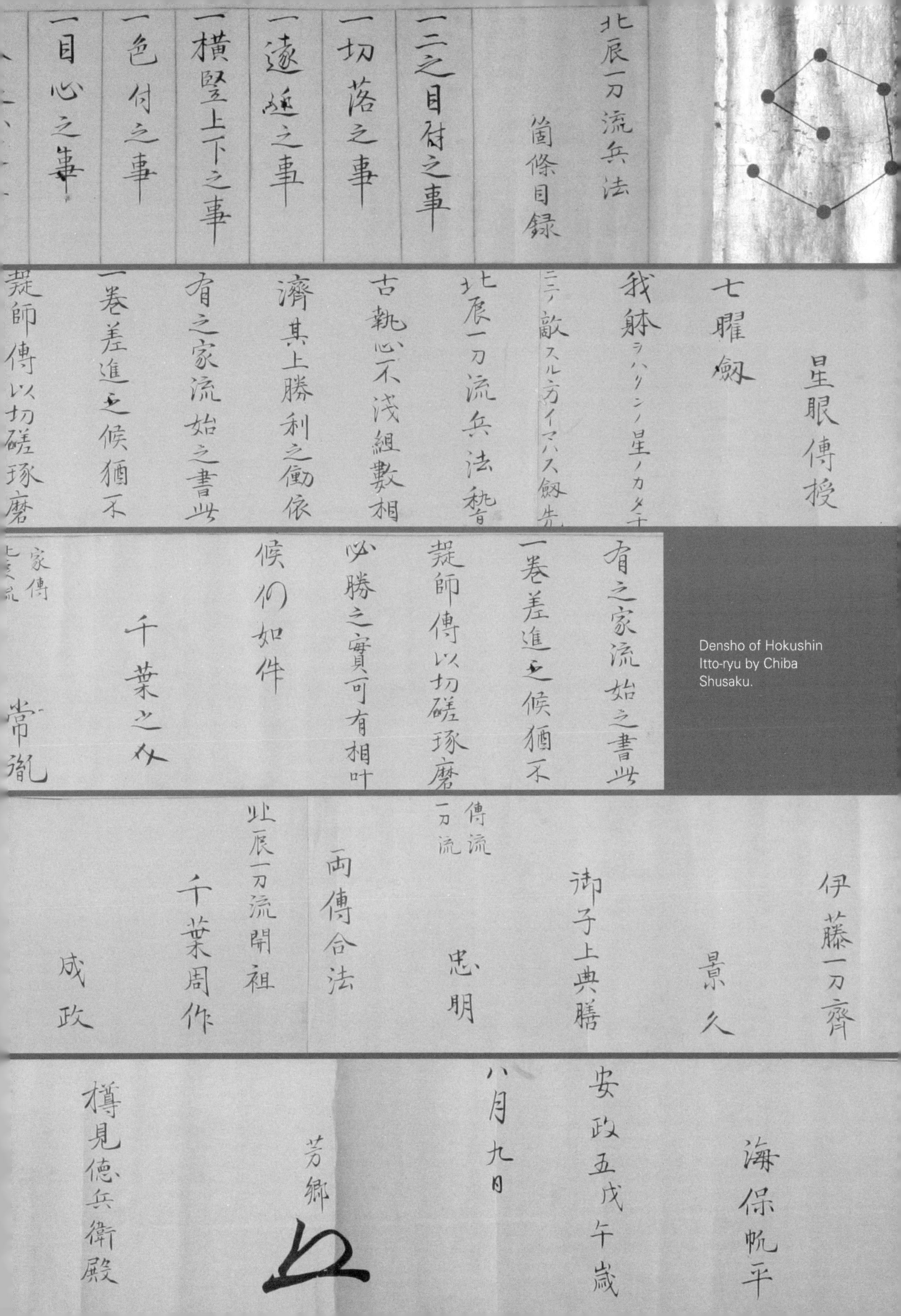

北辰一刀流兵法　箇條目録

一二之目付之事
一切落之事
一遠延之事
一横堅上下之事
一色付之事
一目心之事

星眼傳授

七曜劔

我躰ヲハラフノ星ノカタチ
二ツ敵スル方イマハス劔先

北辰一刀流兵法稽古
擬師傳以切磋琢磨
必勝之實可有相叶

古執心不浅組數相
濟其上勝利之衝依
候仍如件

宥之家流始之書此
一卷差進之候猶不

傳流一刀流

擬師傳以切磋琢磨
一卷差進之候猶不

此辰一刀流開祖
両傳合法

千葉之文
千葉周作

成政
常胤
家傳北辰一刀流

御子上典膳
忠明
安政五戊午歳
八月九日

伊藤一刀齊
景久
海保帆平

樽見德兵衛殿
芳郷

Densho of Hokushin Itto-ryu by Chiba Shusaku.

The Practice of Budo

Toward the True Gokui

There is a tendency to think that the gokui is the ultimate, but this changes according to the subjectivity (shukan, 主観)of the person or the main intuition/sixth sense (shukan, 主勘) of the moment. It is essential to realize this. If you stick to your favorite technique in combat, the opponent will quickly ascertain this, with potentially fatal results. It is therefore important to know that gokui starts from the phenomenon of In and Yo, the balance of opposing forces in the universe. Knowing this phenomenon, the power of In, the advantage of the natural phenomenon of gravity, and being enlightened to this real form, you will begin to understand what the gokui means.

The pursuit of only 'favorite' techniques was admonished as egotistical and self-serving, and these techniques became known as 'tengu waza,' which can be translated into something like 'braggart techniques' (a tengu is a mythical, human-like beast with a long, protruding nose that lives in the mountains. They are often associated with egotism and pride). This is one example of the *Tengu-geijut-suron* (*Discourse on the art of the Tengu*). This book from the Edo period was written by Issai Chozanshi, a retainer of the Sekiyado clan in which tengu speak on the gokui of Budo. Takamatsu Sensei used to say: "People have a tendency to be tengu (highly proud of themselves) in general, but being a tengu is important—from amongst these people are born masters.

Picture of Miyamoto-no Yoshitsune leaping the eight boats continuously, by Tsukioka Yoshitoshi.

Himeji Castle. ▶

It is sometimes acceptable in life to be a tengu; that kind of vehemence might be necessary." This is because fighting means maximizing the free use of a man's weapons and a woman's weapons in all forms. Encapsulated in this is an interest in both sexes (ryosei, 両性) and 'good military strength' (ryosei, 良勢). However, as your boastfulness (tengu, 天狗) increases, do not become a fool (tengu, 転愚). If you drown in lust, you loose your fighting ability.

What I am trying to say is that when you read books like *Tengu-geijutsu-ron* and *Neko no Myojutsu* (*The Cat's Mysterious Skill*)—books regarding Budo—do not get obsessed by them. It is important to clear your head and think simply, just as the word tengu can "change to a fool" (tengu, 転愚). We must not forget that books have the power to brainwash people. It is important not to read with an uncritical eye, and not to believe everything you read. Do not hang everything simply on the contents of a book—just as the tengu can "change to a fool," the cat can lose to a mouse; don't take anything for granted. There are endless kinds of possibilities. Taking the famous book *Hagakure* by Yamamoto Tsunetomo, said to be a book from which you can understand Bushido, you must start by understanding the importance of the questions such as "was the author a Bushi and how much did he understand Bushido?"

There are often two stone guardian lion dogs (koma-inu, 狛犬) placed outside the main building of a Shinto shrine, and these dogs are often called the 'returning lion' and 'facing lion.' One day, one of these guardian lion dogs was stolen from a famous shrine's treasure house. The following day, the remaining koma-inu began to cry at night, causing trouble in the neighborhood. However, after the stolen koma-inu was returned, the crying stopped. The local priest, upon hearing this, began to worship the two koma-inu by praying to them, so their reuniting became a symbol of prayer. I heard that Takamatsu Sensei also made a pair of koma-inu while praying.

I find that the inspiration humans gain from books and the innate connection we share with music have a powerful harmony. When I read Musashi's *The Book of Five Rings*, written about the five elements earth, water, fire, wind, and emptiness, if I put on the jazz CD "Take Five," I can read it in one sitting. Listen to the martial rhyme from the heavenly musical score of chi, sui, ka, fu, and ku. After this, face a piece of paper and paint a picture of Budo or kenpo. Walk the path from martial fighting to martial art and to Bushido, and that path is reflected as the three paths of land, sea, and sky.

By doing this, the popular image of the samurai as depicted in films will disappear. This is not a true image of samurai. If we wish to express zanshin (残心), with a formal understanding it means the state of mental

Densho of Oishi Shinkage-ryu. ▶

大石神影流

刀術截目録 [印]

一 一心

一 無明一刀

一 水月

一 一味

一 順劔

高上

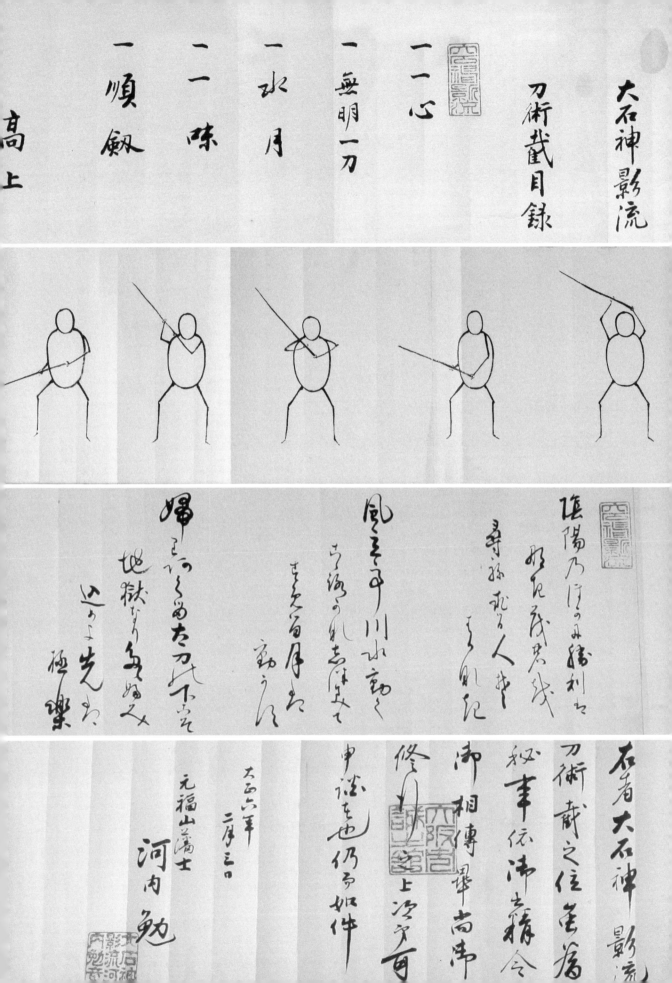

陰陽乃行のみ勝利を
[印]

風
吹きて川水動く
さ波のえ志者えて
まえ名月より
動く月

歸
ふるへるゝ太刀ひ下ふて
地獄なり身ぬゝ又
辻々よ先ほい
極楽

右者大石神影流
刀術截之位爲筈
秘書伝御春令
御相傳譯高弘
修[印][印]上汐□
申述を也仍如件
大西六年 二月三日
元福山満士
河内 勉 [印]

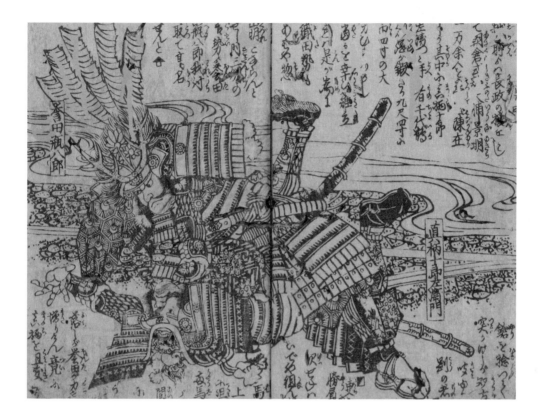

awareness after an attack. However, in the informal understanding it comes to mean 'bold and original' (zanshin, 斬新). If you cannot distinguish the formal from the informal meaning you will not achieve the correct form of zanshin. Practical zanshin of Budo lies somewhere between the previous posture and the subsequent one, in an ethereal, constant state of change.

The 'Niten' of Musashi's *Niten Ichi Ryu* means all things being in flux through the endless circle of birth, death, and rebirth; change again and again (niten 二転, santen 三転); showing the flow that changes in this way. Nature changes because it is beautiful. It is beautiful so it changes. Needless to say, this change must be natural, otherwise a great disaster awaits. The world changes again and again—fertile land is left behind by floods, seeds survive in the earth of an area devastated by fire, allowing flowers to bloom, changing continually.

Large, Small, the Heart, Technique, and Body

There is a famous legend of Issun boshi (the inch-high samurai, a character similar to Tom Thumb in the West). Several years after his birth, Issun Boshi only grew to the size of an adult's little finger, despite being

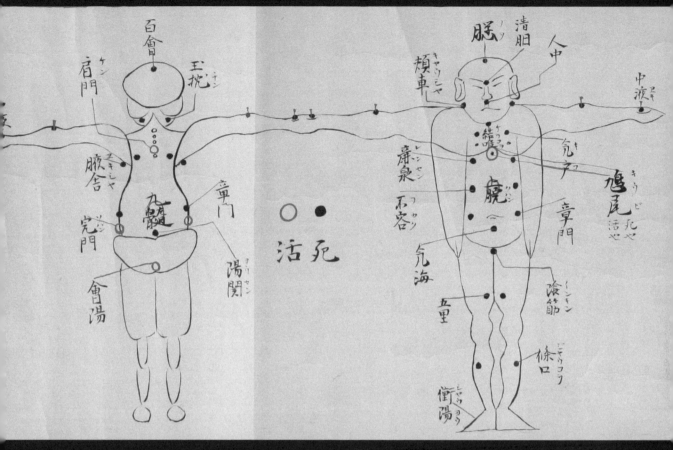

Densho of Shinkyo-ryu.

healthy. He had a dream of going to the city and becoming a samurai, so, using a rice bowl as a boat, he went down the river to the capital. There he was allowed to serve under a well known warrior family. One day, when the princess went to pray at the famous Kiyomizu temple, she was attacked by a large demon. Issun Boshi killed the demon singlehandedly, saving the princess. When the priest of the temple waved the magic hammer left behind by the demon, the diminutive warrior turned into a handsome young man.

When talking about Budoka, the following people come to mind: Judo's Kyuzo Mifune Sensei, Aikido's Morihei Ueshiba Sensei, and Karate's Gichin Funakoshi Sensei. These three men are not very tall, and because they had smaller frames it is said that they had good balance. They also devoted their lives to training, increasing their skills and abilities, and therefore grew to become famous martial artists. Most people who stood in front of these teachers had the impression that they were much larger than themselves. In the same way that there is a long and short sword, there are large and small people. However, through the development of heart, technique, and body (shingitai), both large and small can acquire ability. The greater also serves for the lesser. This means that the Budo of people who know their own values cannot be measured.

Master and Student

At one time Takamatsu Sensei's martial name was 'Chosui' (clear water) and he took great care that his heart and mind were like clear water. This martial name overlaps with the idea in the Japanese proverb "Mizu kiyokereba uo sumazu," meaning, "fish will not live in a stream if the water is too clean." My master took very good care of the divine spring of nature, that is, the flow of clear water. Fish that oppose living in this divine spring, or you might say people who have lost the awareness as Budoka, lose the way of Budo. There is another proverb in Japanese: "San jyaku sagatte shi no kage wo fumazu," meaning "walk three feet behind and do not step on the shadow of your teacher." It would seem that the average person would only accept that this relates to the attitude of the student within the student/teacher relationship. However, how many people realize that it is the master that stands three feet in front of the student protecting the student from an attack from the enemy by using his own shadow as a shield? Furthermore, a teacher is someone that defends tradition. They stand in front, and also look into the future.

I continued training with a mind not to step on the shadow of my master, but after raising students for forty or fifty years there is some-

thing I realized—the real form of the shadow is the very figure of the master. While taking care not to step on the shadow of your master, you may never understand your master's heart. Now I have passed the same age as my master, and I realized that in order to protect my students I must guide them to look ahead. All students need to be protected, not just the good ones. Let us write the character for master (shisho, 師匠) as one who shows justice (shisho, 示正). Among the many kind words that Takamatsu Sensei said, I can recollect a postcard he wrote with the words: "I will make Hatsumi-san a loving pupil." Life is a mysterious thing, and if there is a good teacher and a good student, then life can be continued. If a student that has comparable ability to the teacher is chosen and they succeed the master, they must be careful not to loose the ability that they receive. I received a work of calligraphy from Takamatsu Sensei with the words "ware nashi," which, directly translated, mean "no self." However, it is important to realize that 'ware' (self) can refer also to another person. Failure to understand this means you will not be able to understand your master's words. That is to say, 'ware nashi' can also be heard as, 'no opponent,' or 'no enemy.' Nonetheless, there are times between the student and master when the retainers supplant their lords. However, only the pure relationships survive—it is only a pure and small stream that is alive in the clear vital water.

Speaking of the student-teacher relationship, none had more famous students than Koizumi Isenoka I. His lineup of famous names included: Hikita Bungoro, Jingo Izunokami, Okuyama Kyugasai, Marume Kurando, Yagyu Mitsuyoshi, Matsuda Oribenosuke, Naka Yazaemon, Ashikaga Yoshiteru, and Toyotomi Hodetsugu. Yagyu Mitsuyoshi was later called Yagyu Tajima Nyudo Sekishusa Sogoni after he entered the priesthood. Yagyu Munenori was his fifth son.

Picture of the female warrior Tomoe gozen.

There is a traditional Japanese card game in which one hundred famous poems written by one hundred famous writers are used. The selection of poems is different for every game, and is like a collection of songs of the gokui in relation to Budo and life. Reading this can make you calm and content. This is because songs carry tradition, and within that you can see through to the 'secret' (hiden). The character used for counting poems is written 'shu' (首), which shares the same sound as the word 'neck' (shu, 首). It may be said that in the hundred poems (shu, 首), one may see the hundred heads (necks, shu, 首) of the enemy. Another reading for neck (首) is 'kubi,' which is phonetically the same as 'nine secrets' (kubi, 九秘), or 'eternal secret' (久秘). Incidentally, the character for 'lord' (主) is also pronounced as 'shu.' Yagyu Mitsuyoshi also wrote *100 Songs of the Shinkage*. I possess the book of *100 Songs of Bokuden*, written by Tsukuhara Bokuden. In addition, there is the *Yoshimori Book of 100 Songs*, *Hozoin Book of 100 Songs*, and the *Monster Book of 100 Songs*. The *Book of One Hundred Stories of Demons Traveling at Night* resembles the prayer of *One Hundred Goings* (O-hyakudo Mairi).

Between Densho and Kyojitsu

Densho and Kyojitsu—this means the transmission (densho) and the truth (jitsu) that exists today (kyo) is important. These days, I've come to think that the meaning of densho is connected to the life of the universe. For example, heredity can be defined as not only something between a parent and child but also something between like minded people who are connected to the universe and connected by some bond or destiny, making a transmission that lives on. Without this kind of heredity, would there be transmission (densho) for long? A good example can be found in the scrolls of Budo. Often, between the names of sucessors of the lineage is recorded "generation omitted." This is because the masters recorded had such a strong bond other names in the lineage were omitted. The kyo of the transmission is not falsehood (kyo, 虚), which is the normal reading of kyo, but rather it is real. People thought these masters were legends, but even though they were called 'false,' they passed on genuine techniques to the student, and hence they were in fact real. After being married for a few years but unable to father children, Takamatsu Sensei said to us, "You can still love children even if they are not your own." In Densho and Kyojitsu, nothing more is needed than love.

There is also a form of densho in kabuki. In the region of Edo, correct form was considered a virtue, but in the Kyoto and Osaka regions there was more virtue in the interior expressiveness of the practitioner rather

Picture of kumiuchi.

than the form. In this the kyojitsu that transmits the forms lives. Let me introduce you to two stories of the performances of the kabuki actor Ichikawa Danjuro. The first: in every play there was a scene where Ichikawa Danjuro would sit on a cushion, and the stage hand was appointed to position the cushion wherever he would sit. However, everyday, after the performance was completed, he would complain that the positioning of the cushion was bad, and strike the stage hand. This would continue until one day the stage hand was not struck by Danjuro, so, believing he had found the correct place to position the cushion, he made a mark where he had placed it. He decided if it appeared Danjuro was about to strike him the next day for not putting the cushion in the right place, he would kill him, so he hid a knife in his pouch waiting for the end of the play. However, that day he was not struck by Danjuro. At that point the stage hand suddenly realized and went down on his knees begging for forgiveness. "Master, I'm so sorry," he cried, "I didn't have the ability to see the movement of your performance, I'm only a novice and I'm greatly ashamed to say that I had a thought of killing you master, therefore please punish me in any way you deem necessary!" To this Danjuro responded, "I see . . . well, as you told me I am putting your life on the line in this performance, so don't worry about it."

The second: in a scene where Danjuro was doing a turn, a person skilled with the sword thought if he saw an opening (suki) he would cut him. But there was no opening and his efforts were confounded. From then on he respected Danjuro as a master of the way of the sword. These two episodes are told as parables for building flawless form.

Picture of a wild boar by Takamatsu Toshitugu.

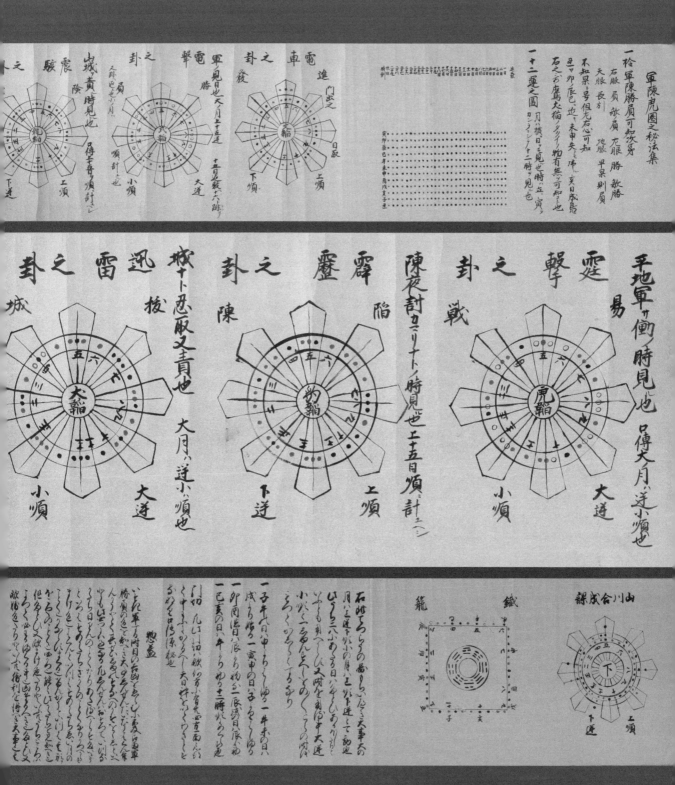

Collection of secret methods of the art of war.
Densho by Koizumi Isenokami.

Budo of Tomorrow

I was once asked: "how do you express in one word practice in the dojo?" I answered, "The dojo is like a pool." You start by getting the people who cannot swim to swim. In this way life can be compared to a pool.

Earlier, I mentioned the work of Fushikaden (*Transmission on the Appearance of a Flower*). My master Takamatsu Sensei sometimes praised "the nature of a flower, the nature of bamboo" (kasei chikusei) and loved flowers deeply. The character for flower is composed of the characters for 'grass in transformation' (花). Perhaps he was comparing a strong life force to flowers or grass. Even if you cut a flower, it will bloom again. Even if it is dried and has lost its shape, if the roots remain, there are many flowers that will bloom again the following year—that is life. As a martial artist, I teach the essence of Budo to people who have the resolution for Budo; I am returning to the spirit of the past. Until now there have been many occasions when I might have lost my life; the fact that I am still alive today must mean that I have a mission in life. Now, having reached the 33rd anniversary of the passing of my master, I have decided to make the soul of Budo known to the world. What is most important is the soul of your fellow man and a mutual feeling toward one another. I think that if the seed of Japan's Budo is planted anywhere in the world, it will continue to grow and flourish.

I never used to think consciously about teaching or

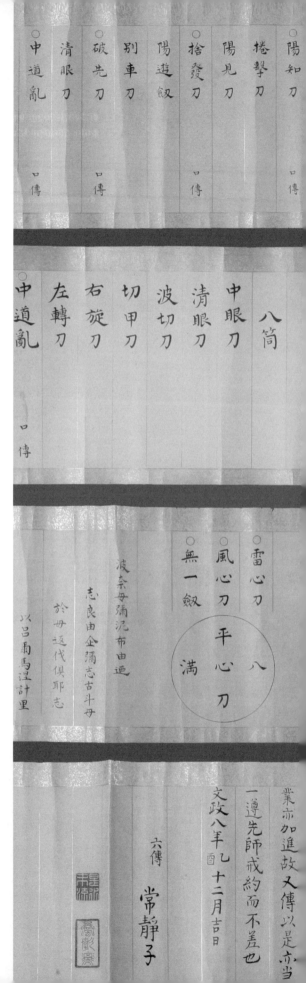

Densho of Shingyo-to-ryu by Matsuura Joseishi. He ruled Hirado as a daimyo and, after retiring, he wrote the famous essay "Kasshi yawa."

心形刀流目録序

夫兵法者心之妙德也故修力
不實更難得本無勝負不求勝
勝自然者也譬如立則有影響
則有響電光石火現於明鏡之
姸媸兵心休自由其味无窮非
言語文字之所及者也平生以
直養之克勉爲表刀之斂也

當流心形刀

○華車刀　口傳
中合刀
中道斂
陰合刀
鎗捨刀
合捨刀
捨輪刀
直和刀　口傳
○獅子亂刀　口傳
虎尾汉

心形刀流諸目録

大亂刀
虎亂刀
○飛龍斂
○九橋刀　口傳
同裏刀
○清眼刀　口傳
○胎內刀
陽重斂
三角切留
發車刀
右斂足
左斂足
陽勇斂
○中道志破記
○膝車刀　口傳
○引疲

古音入門之斂也

一子相傳
水月刀
中道下膝
斂忍試
枕威刀
飛龍斂
龍車刀
初中後陰陽形刀也
右三陰三陽合六箇條本末
條々雖形刀有之當流之極
意者心形刀而已如左

一子不傳

布志遠我牟以我企迺字知泷
彌逗奈礼耶

○清眼刀
○中道亂　口傳

心形刀流之儀依多年修行
今許目録畢假令雖爲兄弟
膠漆之友敢不可謾漏焉若
於執心深首以血印誓約可
有傳授者也

本心刀流元祖
妻片謙壽齋

昔本心刀流也予有志于此術
年久而始似得其妙愿故今改
之號心形刀流

伊庭是水軒　元祖
相傳先師
常全子　二代
常智子　三傳
常機子　四代
常晢子　五傳

spreading Budo around the world. I was just amazed that the world's view of Budo was completely different from my view. At that time I was spurred by the vitality of my youth, and allowed the urge I had to ensure Budo was understood by the rest of the world to drive me. I finally ended this journey and decided not to travel anymore in 2004.

It has been forty-eight years since I met Takamatsu Sensei, during which time I have persevered in the martial ways. There are forty-eight special techniques of Sumo, and I have come to view the number '48' as a martial artist. During my time as a martial artist, with regard to physical techniques, I have no recollection of doing one thing in the same way twice. This represents the 'numerous changes' (banka), of the *Gyokko-ryu Tenryaku no Maki*. The universe is always changing, and this means that I am also participating in the training (keiko) of the universe. Everything in the universe is attracted to everything else by universal gravitation. Time and space; past, present, and future are intimately connected to one another. I feel as though I am now in a time warp. I am walking the narrow path of the world of Gozan literature and haiku, such as recited by the great haiku master Basho:

Summer grass
All that remains
Of the warrior's dreams

The top rank for the Budo Taijutsu of Bujinkan Dojo is 15th dan. There are people who think this is the summit, but a tall mountain is beautiful because it stands in empty space (koku). In the scrolls (densho) of the Gyokko-ryu, the techniques are divided into three sections: joryaku, churyaku, and geryaku. In the scrolls the first method is 'koku,' and is the start of the secret techniques. Now the Bujinkan dojo has spread internationally and Budoka are growing in number. They are understanding the heart of the Budoka bound to the path of the 15th dan. Those who have attained 15th dan often say, "In Japan, there is a ceremony by which a samurai becomes a man at the age of fifteen. I believe we have also reached this coming of age." As for this book, I would like you to read it as a work that can assist you in gaining the knowledge necessary to become an attendee of that coming of age ceremony of the Budoka. It is with this in mind that I have penned my thoughts on these pages.

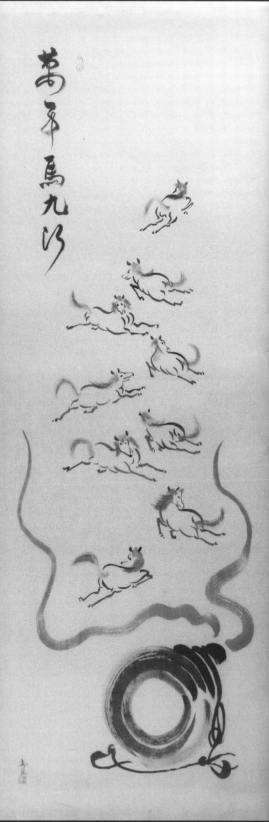

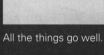

All the things go well.

The passing of the mind into the inner world reveals life's secrets.

Katchu Tachi 甲冑太刀

Katchu Kenpo 甲冑剣法

Catch the opponent's tachi on the shoulder as they cut in from Daijodan. Take the first cut with the sword on the shoulder. Thrust in with the first cut. With the second, cut the throat.

Jinchu no Hira no Kamae (the posture with the sword lowered to the waist level in the battlefield). Against a spear thrust, throw up the thrust and enter with the body. Lift up the spear hand and, catching kote with the tachi, enter in with the body. The important point is to enter with the tachi and body as one.

Kumiuchi Tachi with a whole heart. Take the key point (kaname, 要, and enter into the
key point with 'god eyes' (kaname, 神眼). The kaname defeat the opponent.

Practicing the yama arashi (mountain storm) throw, lift your opponent onto your shoulders. Carrying the warrior is like "carrying one hundred koku (stones)." Crash down the warrior, destroy the opponents as though they are crushed by stones, or smashed by an avalanche.

From Senjin Niten no Kamae. Two heaven strikes (Niten uchi). Cut the opponent's attacking hand with the first strike. Thrusting in with the spear, bring down the opponent's tachi and step on the spear with your right foot. While taking the tachi, kick in and cut into the opponent's vital points.

It is easy **to stab an opponent in armor using a spear**. The spear's superiority in this area meant there was a time it was one of the most common weapons used in combat on the battlefield.

Densho of Muhen-ryu Sojutsu.

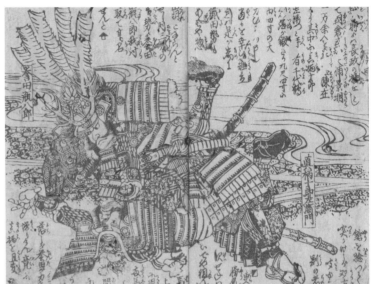

Picture of kumiuchi. Yamanaka Shikanosuke, a
military commander in the late Muromachi period.

Tachi uchi 太刀討

Receive the attack from Hasso no Kamae with the right hand. Strike to the opponent's left side to knock them down. There are many variations after entering with the body. Take the opponent's cut to the left side of the head with the upper arm and shoulder. Lifting in and up with the body, right thurst in with the tachi. Changing the tachi to the left hand, stab in and cut down on the neck.

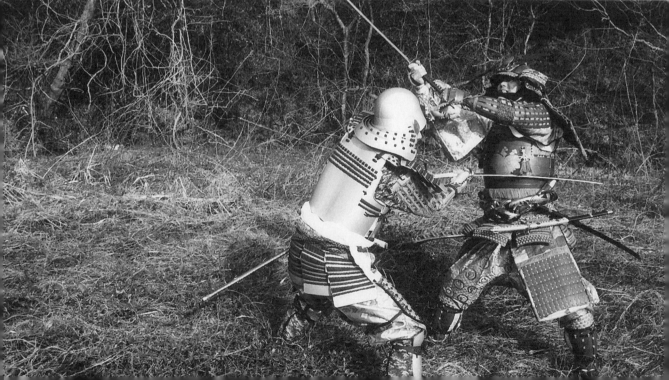

Multiple opponents. The tachi and thrust are one. I repel the opponents' attacks solidly by changing the motion. Six blades: 3 daggers, 3 tachi become all mine. Despite the many opponents, the firm and stable body posture, combined with flexibility, will bring natural victory.

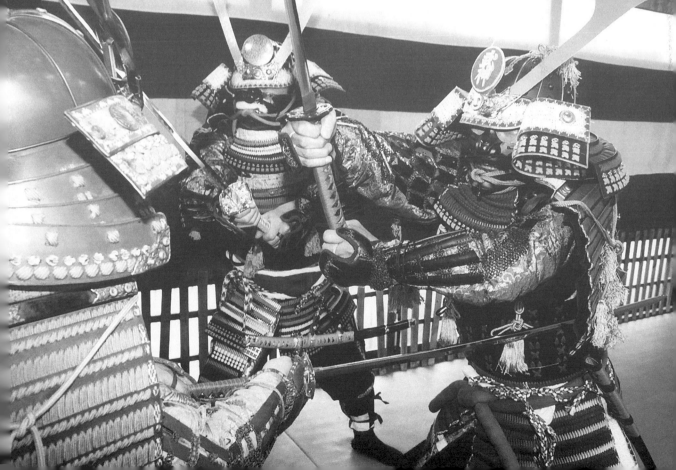

Picture of the warrior Yamanaka Shikanosuke.

Tachi uchi

Yoroi taijutsu

Clothes worn while in the palace or in the castle　殿中衣装

You will easily understand Nanba aruki, the pre-Meiji era style of walking in which the hand and foot on the same side of the body move together, if you wear a long hakama (divided skirt)

大友豊後守義統、緯く、
先祖八鎌倉右幕、将軍らの利朝公ぶ
つり、へうち大友た迎お晴秋速の源瀬
ぎ氏、
氏の春岡
仏仕の氏、
ほしたの俊ぶ
ぞくぐとる其の
孫の自り番ばと
らうひお員て太
隆し傷り、て校
こことねぐぶ太
るぶ閤の先のる
え紀ら男弥三
のふるころ号
えくろ～、き
十二万妖代くの
るーて妖をてける

佐々木六角大膳太夫義秀
多天皇のきる勲月親王作めて
欧頼若祖式部大輔
一頼の秋義婦太
ころ義頼るの祖
あの藤頼座の退
えり高二男三家
の清信が歌の
清四男に佐五郎
の信忍の子の男で
高信の子巧言の男友

「浮舟のごとし」を無刀の心得とする。

波静かなればよく高からばよし。

飛鳥の剣来たるを自然とす忍。

二天一刀二天一流とする。

生位に浮舟にのり敵飛騰を止める。

浮舟の動要に敵動くあたわず。

Understanding muto as "Like a boat floating on water." Whether the waves are gentle or rough, it is good. Hicho no ken (the sword of the flying bird). Regard the opponent's attack as natural. This is Niten Itto, Niten Ichi-ryu. Board the floating boat, and stop the attack. The boat's motion prevents the opponent from moving freely.

Shishiuchi 獅子撃

Stand in Chuseigan with a kodachi. Clad in a long hakama, my attack echoes that of the fierce lion. As the opponent cuts in, step in with a lion's cry. The opponent loses the will to fight as you corner him like a ferocious lion.

Juji Ken (crossed sword) 十字剣

You stand silently in Otonashi no Kamae (the silent posture) with both hands lowered. Even against a strong opponent you maintain this form. The cross-style of this form has a secret meaning that includes both desperation and sacrifice.

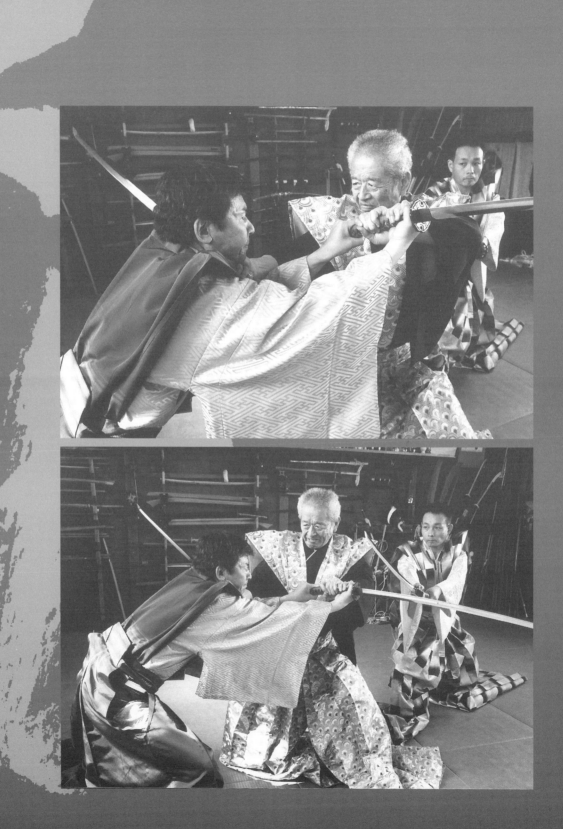

Master Takamatsu Toshitsugu Sensei, Happo Biken

高松寿嗣先生、その八方秘剣

Shinmyoken.

Engekien. San'in no Ote.

Engekien. Komabiki. Hito Takewari. Tsubame gaeshi.

Shinmyo Fudo no ken.

The variation of Gyokute giri Shinmyoken
The sword power that cuts heaven, earth, and man.

Hisho Shinmyoken. Juniten-ho Tsubame gaeshi

By painter Chojin Ookubo (aged ninety-seven).

序文——真の武人たちに捧ぐ

剣聖という言葉がある。それは剣の達人、剣の名人と称される人たちとは異なるものだ。達人、名人といえば、飯篠長威斎をはじめ、愛洲移香斎、上泉伊勢守、塚原卜伝、柳生石舟斎、宮本武蔵、伊藤一刀斎などの名があがる。記録に残っている彼ら剣豪たちは無敗という語り草を繁らせた。その剣技は神業と称され、今日に至るまで名声が轟いている。また富田越後守重政は、前田利家、利長、利常の三代に仕えた武功の人であり、一万三千石の地位に昇った。柳生宗矩は一万二千五百石。ちなみに戦国時代の雄、武田信玄は「人は石垣」と言ったが、米高（米の量）である石とは、サラリーであると共に、地位、国力の象徴であり、経済・権力・武力を表示したものであった。宗矩は将軍・徳川秀忠に新陰流を六年教授し、大目付となる。戦略家としても知られ、幕府が島原の乱の鎮圧に派遣した板倉重昌の戦死を予言するという、武道家として大切な「貫格」（感覚ではない）予知能力にすぐれていた、と草紙に示された。

では剣聖とは何なのだろうか。それは実戦の経験から生まれた剣の道に卓越していたばかりでなく、名人達人をも超越した境地にある人物のことであると私は言いたい。道場で強くとも、合戦に役立つ体験から離れ、真剣勝負に対応できる感覚を忘れた、いわゆる道場剣法や稽古剣法における強者は剣聖の位にはほど遠い。また一考すると、戦国時代末期の頃から、鉄砲が合戦で使われるまでの頃が、もっとも剣の達人が生まれた季節といえる。天下太平の時代ではなく、乱世の「闘争の時代」、すなわち「刀槍の時代」に剣聖が出現しはじめた。

だが、幸運にも生き延び、地位と名声を得ることができた勝者だけが名人と謳われた、そのことを鵜呑みにしては、剣聖の風姿の真実が見えなくなってしまう。世に名前が出なくとも、また今にその名が伝わっていなくとも、じつは彼らに匹敵するだけの実力を持つ、素晴らしい人物たちも存在していたことだろう。そうした剣聖に捧ぐべく、本書を執筆した次第である。

「名人達人といわれていたとて、いったい、いかほどの名人か」と師の高松寿嗣先生がおっしゃられたことがある。勝負に勝ったとか、強者だったとか、それで兵価（評価）することは凡愚なことであり、剣聖といわれる武士、その風姿には、雪月花の起居動作にも似た美しさがある。私が高松先生より九流派の武道を伝授された時の、一瞬の夢を見るような霞（家）伝の映像が、いま幽玄な象となって現れてくる。これぞ宗家と宗家の伝承なのである。その道は自然の誠の道ともいえよう。名人達人は綺羅星のように輝いて見える。しかしながら、剣聖の道は日月のように、師弟ともに色彩を見せるのである。その色彩は、自戒行道に五色の光を放つ。

一、忍耐は、まず一服の間とぞ知れ。

二、人の道に背くことなし。

三、大慾と楽と依怙の心を忘れよ。

四、悲しみも恨みも自然の定めと思い、なお神随（かんながら）の恵みと悟るべし。この神の恵みを見て勘じる時、奇跡という姿を見ることができるのである。

五、心常に宗門、武門の道に離れず、深く文武に志すべし。

この五定、確と守る事大事。

　ここにある、志すという字を、士の心と両眼で見られるようになれば、葬儀の時、仏に畏敬の念をもって香典を供する士の心を「武士道とは死ぬことと見つけたり」の一節として解釈でき、また介錯の情けをも知ることもできるのである。剣聖への道、剣の道を歩もうと思う人ならば、この格言を大秘として、武風一芸、この道をしっかりと歩んでいただきたいものである。

第1章　武道における日本剣法

武道における日本剣法

　刀はよく斬れるものと思われている。しかし相手が鎧武者の場合など、斬れるはずの刀が斬れない場合がある。戦国時代終わりの頃には、時の流れは、刀を狩り捕る刀狩りの時代へと変わった。ペンは剣よりも強し、やがて刀剣は美術工芸品として生き残ったものの、剣法家を風化させ続けてきた。真剣を用いた本当の時代を生きぬと、その事実がわからない。かつ本当の武道家のことを知らないから、そういう考えが生まれてもこない。だから本当の武道を理解してもらうために、一番ピークと言われた、上泉伊勢守、塚原卜伝をはじめとする、室町時代へとタイムスリップしてみよう。

　組討ちの時代を生きた武士ならば、太刀の長短、その技法について、斬る、突く、叩く、ということを組討ちの途上で発見したものである。私たちは、この時代の経験が剣法を生んだということをまず知るべきである。また、刀に頼らない格闘技を乱闘の中で悟った。南北朝から室町時代、戦国時代にかけての下克上の風潮のなかでは、武士道の風媒花が咲き乱れ、桜のごとく散り、また四（士）月の桜が咲いた。

　そこには鮭にも似た姿がある。鮭は激流に立ち向かい、川をさかのぼり、産卵し、受精をし、闘いつつ死んでゆく。次の世代を生きる者のための自然からの天命が見てとれる。それは、参年（まいねん）、氏尊（しそん）、家名を残すために激闘して力尽き、死んでいった武士たちの姿と重なる。その天命が室町時代に下り、武士たちの世界をもっ

とも美しく表現している。室町時代こそ、自然の武情の出発点である。それは禅文化、五山文学、剣禅一如にと受精させた時代である。と同時に、それは幽幻から花の世界へと向かう時代でもあった。そのひとつ能も、花道へと至る高野聖の影響を見てとれる。

　室町時代、一休宗純たちの禅僧によって五山文学が花開いた。時を同じくして能、茶道、華道も生まれた。それらは将軍など権力者の庇護のもとに発展を遂げた。とはいうものの、当時、絶対的象徴であった将軍の権力に逆らう芸風の権力は、問答無用の一喝のもとに両断されてしまった。能の世阿弥は、将軍の勘気を被り、島流しにあったが、なぜ、世阿弥は自らが説いた「秘すれば花」という幽玄の世界を、将軍の権力の前で艶（演）じなかったのだろうか。芸の魂というものは、鬼籍に本籍があると強く思える。茶道の千利休はもともと鬼籍の人だという人もいるが、将軍に代わる権力を握った太閤秀吉の勘気をかい、鬼籍に帰っていってしまった。芸には権力者の力が及ばない別世界がある。従って権力者は武芸者をも恐れた。しかし一人武芸者は五定を護り大悟する、唯一無二の人となりであった。そこに剣禅一如の思想が生まれたのは当然のことであろう。鬼籍の鬼は神の裏字ともなっている。即ち鬼籍とは、神界を指すこともある。神籍とも表示されるからだ。

戦わずして剣の道の神価を行く

　幕末から明治にかけて活躍した剣豪・榊原健吉。直新影流の達人と言われ、兜割りで知られる。だが、兜が少し斬れたからといって、たいしたものだとほめそやすのはおかしい。兜を斬りたいのならば、大斧や長刀で叩き割ったほうがよい。七つ道具のひとつ大斧を使えば簡単に割り斬れるだろう。これが軍略兵法である。

　刀の五囃とは、ご神体と畏敬、祈念、弥栄、ヤ・エイの気合いと共に神結びをするものだ。ご神体を一刀両断することなく一刀ご神体に収め、一刀神殿に誓い、許され、納刀をする。

　剣豪として、また剣禅一如の思想と雄渾な書で知られるのが、明治天皇の教育係として十年間勤めた山岡鉄舟である。猛訓練と大悟の末に、とうとう道場で、師の浅利又七郎と勝負を離れ、真の勝負をし、剣の道を知ったと伝えられている。大悟し、その神歌を心に聞き、自覚したと見るべきである。「強弱柔剛あるべからず。故に此の心を離れ、空の一字を悟り、体又無しとして、これに配す」という極意の歌がある。それを禅味によって聞くことができたのであろう。そして大海原に浮く鉄の舟、鉄舟は波浪を切り進んで、一刀流の極意へと開眼し、極意の詞韻を聞いたのであろう。――「身の備え　勇を表わす武の中に　真の極意は心なりける」「抜かず勝て　抜けば切るなよ　ただ忍べ　命をとるは大事とぞ知れ」。

　2004年の冬、野田の琴平神社の大祭で弟子たちと共に演武を奉納した。「神結び」という言葉の、試し切りの演武である。二本スパスパと四方斬りに斬ったが、

　五本目神結びの五本目は斬らせなかった。神様に奉納するとき、全部斬ってしまうと、神縁を切ることになるからである。知らない人が見ると、「なんだ、最後は斬れないじゃないか」と言うが、そうではない。「仏に逢うては仏を斬り、神に逢うては神を斬り、しかる後に極意を得ん」というような劇の台本ではないのだから、神との結び誓いを斬るような不心得なことは許されぬのが武風なのである。

勝負の本質

　武道というのは絶対に勝つという予知能力が大事であり、絶対勝つという心構えからは迷いが生じない。人間というのは、程度の差はあっても、誰しも勝ちたいという気持ちがほとんどであろうが、その戦う様を古い文献は、虎擲龍挐十方折衝の術として、大自然が猛狂う中で、龍と虎の戦いとして表現している。稲妻の光が雷雲、雷雨を生かし、風の音響も加わって、驚愕の美的効果を上げていく。その場面に踏み込んだ六感は同化される。相手に勝ちを譲っても、自分にプラスになるという計算とかゆとりがある人ならば、勝ちは譲る。これは自然の法則に過ぎぬものだが、煩悩に溺れるものは、それに気づかないものである。ギブアンドリターンというか、中里介山式に「輪廻」と言っておこう。ただし、ここで大切なのは、実戦では、勝負を生死に置き換えることである。自分に対してゆとりが持てたら、生命力が強くなる。それには沈勇を養うことだ。

　戦いによって勝者と敗者が生まれる。ほんのわずかなことから、常勝の強者をも敗者へと導く。それが道場剣法ではなく、真剣勝負ならば、さらに明らかなものとなる。いうまでもなく、竹刀ならば一二発打たれようが突かれようが構わないが、真剣ならば命を失ってしまう。だが真の武人は、真剣勝負でもこだわらず、臆することなし、という心構えを養うのである。なぜか。それは勝敗というこだわりから離れた悟閃賦の生命線に立っているからだ。音とは五線譜、すなわち五輪の書からも飛び出ている生命の響きである。

　私のもとで二十年間、稽古を続けている某国の元軍人がいる。彼は先日、テロと流血にさらされている現代の世界情勢に触れて、こんな手紙をよこした。「実戦を経験した軍人として、私はいかなる戦争においても、勝者はひとりもいないと確信しております。本当のところ、すべてが敗者であることを感じております。勝者とされている者でさえも、降伏して手をついた敵の血に取りつかれ、遅かれ早かれ、苦しむことになるでしょう」と。勝敗にとらわれる者は、勝敗にいつまでも苦しめられる。

　人類の間で戦争が消え去ることはないのだろうか。それを考えて消えたのが忍者であった。またその心構えにならって極意とし、神に誓って、神の影を極意とし神妙剣を生んだのである。なぜ自然の生命は闘い合うのだろうか。自然淘汰、この四文字を自然闘多に置き換えて考えたとき、人類の命の性の引き合うミステリーがドラマ化された大河を見る思いがするであろう。

宗教と武道

　人類に生まれた原人は約二十、その一つ、狩人であるクロマニオン人（ホモ・サピエンス）だけが生き延びた。しかし、クロマニオン人がいちばん死霊についておびえてきた。これは、今で言う宗教観の深層にある死に対する防御反応、そのことを自然に感じさせる奥境観にタイムスリップしたものであろう。

　言葉でコミュニケーションをとり、長時間走り回りながら、集団で動物と戦い、血にまみれた肉を食した、そのクロマニオン人だけが生存しているという説を借りれば、現代人に言語能力、走るなどの身体能力、集団能力、そして闘争本能があるのも、祖先が獲得し、発達させたものだという。狩猟民族だからこそ武器を使い、罠を使う。従って自然淘汰とはすなわち自然闘多なのであろう。武道の大事さはそこにある。武道とは生きることである。獣道などを思っていると、道からはずれるが、人道的感覚では狩りはできない。

　もはや地球上の人類は過剰である。世界の人口は、現在の64億人から、2050年には約91億人に増大するという。そのため天門地門の自然闘多の現象へと変化があろう。地震や、火山の噴火、津波、洪水などの天災が来るのも神の啓示であり、そのことを自覚しなさい、と師の高松寿嗣先生はいわれた。それらは元はといえば、生物が忍耐と洞察と自然の本体をつかまずに、地球の環境を破壊していることからきているのだから、自然を恨むことはできない。自然体が世界をこういうふうに創り、人類の犯していることが人類に返ってきたのだから、本を正せばよい。give and returnであり、自然に対して良いことをしていれば、自然から人間は大事にされ、良いことを返されるのである。

　地球の温暖化ということが言われているが、寒暖計を頼りにしていると、生命の危機は自覚できないものである。自然生物のもつ「勘断計」をもっと大切にすることである。自然形態は、自然帯に結ばれながら生き続けている。武道で言う自然の構えも、それに匹敵した自然体なのである。

　武道も同じであろう。それが「武心、和をもって尊しとなす」という「銘鏡」なのである。だから逆に言えば、武道家は宗教家、哲学家、思想家の感覚と超感覚の科学的変化化学のプロフェッサーということになる。「化」という字から「花」「靴」「貨」「傾」という字が生まれる。化けパズルである。「家」の廻りに宗教哲学思想政治をつけたら、と剣聖は考える。宗教思想哲学が原因となって戦争が起きるが、武道は「三家」（宗哲思）もガードしなければいけない。そうでないと人類が滅びてしまう。そういう武道観が、いずれごく当たり前のこととして受け止められることだろう。童話のごとくに。『グリム童話集』が一例で、童話というのは時に非常に恐ろしい、悲惨なことが秘められている。お母さんたちは、そのことに気づかずに、子供たちに読んで聞かせている。防御本能を生かして解釈したら、残酷な話に気づいてくるものである。

　ここで残酷という言葉を自然の流れとして見つめることができる。そんな眼で、

　残酷という二字から虹を見る骨法と思うことである。バラ色の人生と言うが、生老病死、そこにもバラが咲いている。

　残酷といえば、神の教えも、本当は厳しく残酷なものだ。だからこそ、それぞれの時代に聖人が出てくる。イエス・キリストにせよ、ムハンマドにしろ、釈迦にしろ、ほぼ同時代に現れたというところが興味深い。さらにいえば、プラトンや、老子、荘子、孔子もその前後に生涯を送った。変革の時代が偉才を必要としたのである。

　では、私たちが淘汰（闘多）されるのを避けるにはどうすればよいか。極意の唄にもあるように、ただ斬る者を相手せぬ術とはモハトマ・ガンジーが唱えた無抵抗主義なのかもしれない。

　『忍者の道』の本で、庭と忍者（武道家）と文化が三位一体である三才の法を知り、参考になったという声が寄せられた。庭の中でも、白砂を山化、川化、海化、池化し、大自然の美を現出する「枯山水」の庭園は日本文化の極致のひとつである。ところが残念なことに、現代の日本では、いわゆる日本庭園をもつ家がじつに少なくなった。庭園づくりと庭園の維持には予想以上の費用がかかるから、ふつうの生活力では維持できず、断念してしまう。傾（かぶく）である。だが、知ってほしい。文化の継承発展、維持には経費がかかるのは当たり前なのである。文化芸術を知り尽くしてこそ武道家である。そうすれば、勝負も生死も達観できる。すなわち識（しき）をしのぶことのできる武人だ。識とは死悸を護る、そして志気、傾（かぶ）くを護る、永遠に伝統を守る美意識でもある。

一元それは万変して乱れ帰る

　密教では地水火風空の五つの要素の他に、識（しき）（色）を見ることができる。忍法では「しき」で忍ぶというが、曼荼羅の色が見える。墨絵の時代を過ぎ、いまはカラーの時代である。しかし、黒には五色ありというではないか。その五色とは、虹の七色をプラスして十二色となり、年の過ぎゆく様が見えてくる。地水火風空を謡の「卒塔婆小町」では「五輪は人体」と言っている。ここに大乗小乗の五輪の変幻を見ることだ。遠くオランダの画家ハルスは黒で二十七の色を出す。いうなれば、二と七の九字の色は、画家の誓いの色だったのだろう。多彩は多才なり。

　軍略兵法家は、博く物事を見、かつ考えるものだ。一つのものには裏表があると同時に、五大、六大（六界とか六波羅蜜とか六具）、さらに七大、八大（武道には基本八方がある）がある。だから世の中は奇計奇妙なのである。六道を超えたところに、七つ目の虹の道がある。だが、その虹に染まってしまうと危険だ。だから七（しち）という数字は日本では凶とされている。

　一元とは四万の法十法に続く四万十川なのであろうか。従って武道を学ぶことによって、万元に続く。それは武道とは限らない。宗教でも学問でも同じだろう。私はけっして武道が最高のものだとは思わない。この地球で存在しているものの一つ

だと思う。「万物は帰一す」という言葉がある。丸に一の字（⊖）を書く。これもシンボルのひとつであろう。禅では「接待」を指す。達磨絵も、もともとは達磨大師の姿を写実したものだったのが、だんだんと抽象化していき、やがて丸になり、全相を見ることができるのである。

武芸十八般の本当の意味

　私が最近とくに痛感しているのは、何の芸術でもそうだが、一貫することの重要性である。「師匠が馬の尻尾につかまっておれば、虫けらやかて、千里いけるのやさかい。頑張りなさい」と、師の高松先生が四十八年前に言われたことが昨日のように思い出される。「そうだ、馬は千里行く、そして猛古虎（師の武名）は千里帰るという諺があるなあ」と亡き師と言葉を交わしたものだ。今私はクッキーというミニホース（小さい馬）と住んでいる。十数年前から馬の絵を描いているのだが、ときどき手を加えていたものの、なぜかその絵が気に入らない。ところがクッキーと同居してから、その絵を完成することが出来たのである。八法秘剣といわれた時代の九数から月日の日月が十八般を生んだのである。18は1＋8で9なのである。そして18÷2＝9であり、2とは陰陽阿吽である。

　「歌舞伎十八番」「武芸十八般」という言葉がある。それぞれ「歌舞伎の代表的十八作品」「主要な武芸十八種類」を意味する。武芸十八般といえば、體術、剣術、棒術、槍術、居合術、馬術、手裏剣術、捕縛術などを思い浮かべられることだろう。ここで歌舞伎十八番について武芸者の見方を語ろう。歌舞伎華やかな頃、団菊左（市川団十郎、尾上菊五郎、市川左団次）の時代があった。この三人の舞台は一世を風靡するものがあった。十八とは、これを三人が六方を踏んだとき、十八の和が調和し名武体が艶じられたのである。十八番は一番槍の話にも通じた語り草ともなっている。

武道の王政復古

　人生は一瞬である。その一瞬に生きることを生涯の「一悟一会」として尊び、大自然の中に生かされている天佑に感謝し、命あるすべての存在をいとおしみ、一瞬の中に永遠性を見いだし、幸運にも人生の年輪を重ねて円熟を堪能することのできた者の作品には蘊蓄がある。

　能の秘伝書として有名な『風姿花伝』（世阿弥作）に「秘すれば花なり。秘せずは花なるべからず」という言葉がある。日本の武道の根底をなす日本文化に住みついた仏教で大切にされている「一隅を照らす」ことに通じるのは興味深い。威風堂々とした黄金の仏像と対照的な、素朴な円空や木喰上人作の仏像の微笑みが「風天の寅」に見せる愛を感じる。

　歴史の浅い武道観だけで説明すると、武道の妙味を失う。そんな時、維新にみせた王政復古の鼓笛のリズムに耳を傾けてほしい。秘められた武風は、温故知新の道をたどりながら、管仲のいう老馬に乗って聞いていただきたいと思う。武道というものは、新しいものばかりを追っていると、大切な秘文を見捨ててしまうからである。王政復古とは、往生復呼なのである。「太陽の光を浴びて生きていこうよ。『ユーアーマイサンシャイン』を唄おうよ。武道を修業して笑顔を忘れてはいけない」ということを諭しているのだ。どんなことがあっても驚かずに完爾としていよ、という気合いがあるからである。

武道と芸術

　武士の豊饒は、鎧甲などの武具を工芸的にも美しいものとし、またその権力を誇示するために、金閣寺、銀閣寺や黄金の茶室を造ったといわれるが、権力者の秘意識と美意識のなせる業かもしれない。鉄砲が入ってきて急速に、刀の実用性は、武士道を駆ける者を標的とした。炎の中から見つけられた武士道は、戦国時代に燃え尽きたのである。そのとき既に、世界的に共通の価値のある物は、金剛石と呼ぶダイヤモンドであるということを知っていれば、侍の社会もだいぶ変わったのではないかと思う。仏像の眉間にある、いわゆる第三の目に嵌め込まれたダイヤモンドやルビーなどは、仏像の意識を示したものかもしれない。信長、秀吉は、武将たちに恩賞として、何万石、何十万石を授ける代わりに、名刀や匠味の者を与えた。茶碗はダイヤモンドと同等だった。

　ヘレーネ・クレラ・ミュレー（オランダの画家）は「芸術とは人間の形を魂としたものだ」と語ったという。では、武士の魂を見るためには、そして大和魂を見るためには、どうすればよいのだろうか。それは武芸を習得した武芸者の象^{かたち}から見て取れるのではないだろうか。そうしてこそ武道家という存在を自他共に見られるようになるだろう。

　幻想的な日本画を描いた速見御舟（1894-1935）は、「私は一生型を破壊していくかもしれない」と語って、伝統的な日本画を破壊させながら描き続けた。それが彼の芸術の本質だ。破壊の表現が変わるかもしれないが、モンドリアンの画風も、禅画に見る画風も、芸術というものは自然に風化させているのである。わびさびと共に同居するように、造化の天工のなせる風天護身反応汎溢の自然力が剣聖には同化するのである。

極意とは何か

　極意は変化とともに生きているものだと私は思う。人も変われば物も変わり、時代の状況も変わるからだ。それぞれの時代に極意というものがなければおかしい。

　だが、いつになっても変わらない、時代が変わっても不変の、本質的な極意こそが本当の極意だと思う。武道は何千年前からあるが、私の武道が世界に通じているということは、やはり私が極意的なものの中に生存していることを示しているのだと思う。だから、極意というのはこういうものか、とわからなくても、良師畏友と結ばれながら武風一貫していればよい。

　五九五と数解きをすると、五は神代の最高の数であり、九は今とすれば、次に古き良き経験が生じる。この数の変化に極意を見ることができる。

　しかし大切なものは、再度言うが、極意とはあるかと思えばなし、ないかと思えば極意は奇跡のごとく鬼籍の中から現れる。極意という存在はミステリアスなものだ。

　人には器がある。それが現実だ。落語家の柳家小さん師匠も言っていたではないか。大切なのは学ぶことだが、どんなに学んでもダメなら、それだけの器ということである。だから歌舞伎役者でも、跡継ぎや弟子に全然教えない人もいる。それでいて、伝統の芸を見事に継承していく名人も出てくる。

　武士道には功名はつきものである。そのために、「武士道とは死ぬことではない」と言うと、「死を恐れているのではないか」と早合点する者が多いが、武士は最後まで忍耐ということを掟としたものである。憤死してはもったいないということを知ってほしい。ゴッホ、モーツァルトといったたくさんの有能な芸術家の死を見ると、惜冬の思いがする。「窪地へと落ちる習いの水なれど、やがては登る始めなりけり」の神韻を聞いてほしいものだ。自然のまま、生老病死を超越してこそ武士の心意気が後世に語り継がれるのである。私は師伝武風を伝授され、超越の中に兆悦という天国を見たからである。世に認められないからといって死に急ぐことは、天命に非することになる。才能ある者の悲しい一刻である。

　生命力というのは、確かに自分でコントロールし、養っていくものだが、それだけではない何かがある。私が神棚にお供えをあげていたら、ろうそくの炎の関係で、十文字の光が神棚にぴたっと映っていた。不思議だなあと思って師匠にたずねたら、「ああ、あんたは、宇宙の何かと結ばれている」と言われたものだ。このように自然からの直観が大切であるということを感じとってほしい。

　私の場合は、師の言われた一言一言が、私を運行させてくれていた。それが自然なことなのだ。そして自分で事を為せばよいと思っている。それには「悸」がある。そこに「極意の引き合う力」が見えてくる。持って生まれた器でない者にやらせようということは神の意に反すると、この頃いたく感じてきた。神結びのためには、神ながらは師ながらの同じ流れに生きることだ。

常識から超越する

　私は文献に対しては、美術刀剣を見るごとく、すべてとはいわないが、即断定はしないことにしている。瞬間の光で眼をつぶらせることがあるので、瞬間それに従

わないこともある。今や易や占いのブームだが、断定するのは失敗の初めである。不明の事柄の正体を断定せずに、曖昧なままにしておくことは、美化して言えば、幽玄の世界と繋がってくるものである。物事を煙にまく「煙」にしても、たくさんの種類がある。公害の煙もあれば、仁徳天皇の煙や忍者の煙もある。

　ある武道研究家が、「いろいろな流派のことを研究し、本を出版したが、結局何にもならなかった」と私に言ったことがある。私はそれに対して、「何にもならなかったことがわかればいいじゃないですか。それが万物が帰一するという言葉なのだから」と言ったものだ。じつは武芸についても同じことがいえる。「研究しても何にもならないことがわかる」ことが、絶対的に大切なポイントなのである。帰一について言えば、1それは0を要に、＋1と－1があり、プラスとマイナスがあるから、1を知れば即ち陰陽を知ったことになり、立派なものだ。

　武道というのは、生きる心得であり、識を知る心構えでもある。識とは四季であり、指揮、死悸、士気、詩悸、士器という形象でもある。

　歴史の通説や文献に頼ってしまうと、歴史の真実が見えなくなってしまう。しかも歴史には異説、奇説がさまざまに混在し、新説も次々と生まれ、何が本当かはわかりづらくなっている。そうした一般的な常識や諸説をいったん捨て去り、本当の姿を見据え、そのエッセンスを本書では表現しようとしている。とはいえ、それは本当の修業をした者でなければ、なしえないことである。

　平泉中尊寺貫首となり、一時は国会議員も務めた、人情の機微を解し人間的魅力あふれる作家、今東光大僧正（1898–1977）は色紙に「真心是道場」という言葉を記した。そう、まごころこそが、善からも悪からも、生からも死からも、勝敗からも、運不運からも超越できるのである。これは武道の極意に通じる至言である。

第2章　日本剣法の本質

押し切りの刀法

　古代には武器というものはなかった。剣とか弓矢だけは古くからあったが、酋長とか一部の長のみが帯していたらしい。紀元前500年頃、外国から渡来した者たちが倭国に対し戦いを挑んだ折り、組討、棒、石投、弓矢をもって敵の攻勢を防ぎ、また壕を造り戦ったと古書にある。後年には他国からもたらされた武器と類似の武器を造り、発達した。やがて武器の使い道も進歩して、徳川時代には武器の技術は実に百二十通りといわれ、寛永時代より徳川末期においては三千以上の流名が現われたという。

　古代の棒刀から剣が生まれ、その剣は太刀へと発展し、そして刀として変化した。戦国時代にポルトガルから種子島に伝来し、またたく間に日本中に普及した鉄

砲の威力はだれもが知り、弓刀槍にまさる武器として認められていたにも拘わらず、鉄砲が刀より上位に置かれることは一度たりともなかった。なぜだろうか。それは刀とはけっして殺すのが目的ではなかったからである。

　刀とは支配階級がもつ権威であり、心を護るシンボルであり、野蛮な殺人者であってはとうてい持ち得ないシンボルであった。人を殺すための武器でありながらも、安心立命を護るための本尊でありシンボル、その二面性（二極に生きる生命）をもつところに刀の最大の特徴がある。

　竹刀はいつ頃から出来たか、木刀はいつ頃から出来たのか、そして剣は、太刀は、刀は、いつ頃出来たのかという問いに対し、一般的には分類し説明するのが丁寧なことだと、曲（もの）を教える人は確信しているが、武道家はそんなことは考えていない。武道の根本はまず、物、武器をもたずとも戦えるという體術を会得することが大切だと師伝されている。武風一貫、一生懸命修業することだ。そこに、無刀捕の秘術を会得でき、その暁に秘剣の奥義を見せられるようになるのだ。どんな武器をもとうが、心と體術とが琢美（たくみ）に、虚空を舞うようになる。そこで竹刀について、木刀について、語り伝えることができるのである。

　ここで竹刀武勇伝を語ろう。大石進という、五尺あまりの竹刀を使う、左突きの名手がいて、江戸の名のある道場に他流試合を申し込んでは、次々と短い竹刀を持った剣客を倒していった。そこで講武所では、竹刀の長さを三尺八寸に決めたともいわれている。また明治の時、学生たちの剣道大会で、竹刀の長さを決めずに試合をさせていた時、竹刀の長い方が勝つ確率が高かったので、竹刀の長さを一定したともいわれている。その昔、長短槍試合で、長い槍のほうが強いという説話が残されているが、このような単純なことで、勝負という、未知との遭遇を参考にするのも、勝負と真剣型のバランスを計る口伝となるものである。

　さて廃刀令が出された明治期の1912年に制定された、竹刀や木刀を用いるスポーツとしての剣道とは異なり、「即、突き、胴」の動作で決まる真剣の場では「押し切り」の刀法でゆく。すなわち、型を超えた実戦的な世界である。相手が刀ごとぶつかってきた時に自分の刀を引くと、相手の刀と身体が入ってくるから、押して倒すようにするのだ。実戦では刀で斬られたのがわからずに反射的に斬り込んでくる人の姿も見受けられる。押し切りの方が危険度は少なく、押し切りは心得である。

　真剣、竹刀、木刀でも、武人は弘法筆を選ばず。何故かといえば、無刀取りの心得があるからだ。虚空に潜む変化に応じ、変に順じ、虚に順じ、刀を用い、敵に対するのは、けっして敵を殺害し、味方の侵略を利するためのものではない。「妙風剣」「真剣白刃取り」の真義は、これに順じ応じていく24コマの光と影を写し出す。

武具の化粧、言い換えれば魂の美化
　戦場で侍たちは、鎧兜を身に着けた。それは40キロぐらいの重さがあった。す

　ると、その鎧兜をまとった體術というのは、今の柔道などの体の動かし方とは違ったものである。重さを感じさせない、そこにコツがある。もっとも、現代の軍人たちも重装備したらすごい重さになる。40キロどころではない。だから、鎧兜による體術、体変術は実は現代が求めているものでもある。

　鎧兜で身を固めた武者と戦う場合、一太刀で斬り込むということは至難の技であり、抜群の力量を要する。そこで組太刀、組討ち體術の必要性が生じてくる。一番目の太刀から、二番目の太刀で鎧の弱所空隙を突き斬り込む。三の太刀で止める。または、一番の太刀で突き打ち叩く。組討ちに入りつつ太刀で突き叩き斬る。打ち倒し、首を捕る。また槍や長刀をもってしても同様である。

　闘う者たちの明暗が、傷の深さ浅さによって決められていき、深手を負った者には「傷は浅いぞ」と励まし、浅手を負った者には「なんぞこれしきの傷」と励ましたものである。この励励の言葉がレイの音を発し、九字の一言となっている。

　武将は鎧兜を身につける。それは美しいものである。人間は顔を化粧するだけでなくて、心から化粧するものだ。着ているもの、そして武器まで化粧する。つまり美の世界、虚無美の世界ということだ。化粧には、美と醜と、変化戦略が潜んでいる。昨今、嘘という言葉が流行っている。たとえば誰かが死んだとしても、それを嘘だと思うことがオーバーラップした話戯復活がある。生命の維持を助けるために、嘘という手段を使うこともある。演劇にせよ音楽にせよ、約束事を設けて出発するものの、より良い作品を作るために、嘘を練り込んで完成させたりする。最高ではないが、時代背景の危険から脱して人の心を打つ作品となるものがある。嘘から出た真が、人間の深奥に潜んでいる心に達することができるからだ。これは以心伝心の腹芸の一つになっている。芝居で見る勧進帳や忠臣蔵の一場面を見ても、うなずけることと思う。

　宮本武蔵の遺体は、生前の希望に基づき、鎧兜を着込んだ正装で、立ったまま埋葬されたと伝えられている。そのエピソードから、死後も武人であり続けたいという話戯が復活して生き続けるのであろう。

槍と刀の関係

　槍術が確立したのは戦国時代だという。この時代には、鎧兜を身楯として戦う武者姿の隙魔《すきま》を突き倒す、叩き倒す、斬り倒すには、槍が有利であったということを知った上で、八方秘剣一如となって戦う武者姿の映像を見た時、はじめて剣の道が発見されるのである。そこで刀槍の道をたどってみよう。

　人類は、長い柄物に、先のとがった形状をつけて、獲物を突き刺したり、土を掘ったりすることを発見した。遣り手エイプマンこそ、槍術家原人と称してもよいだろう。槍の歴史、発生については諸説あるが、槍術が非常に多く使われ、テクニック的にも上昇したのは、主に戦国時代と言われているが、私の修得した流

技は、古くから槍術を秘伝として伝えている。その一つとして、こんな記録が残されている。「紀元前550年、仏教徒、吠檀達、磯城に住してから、入鹿の当時、七千五十三戸、二万数千人の吠檀達となれり、勢力あなどり難し。故に統一に困難なること、慮り、神等集まり、議り給うて、尪法の用意を設けらる。

尪法とは、九つの武器の法である。

一、築城	石塀、石室のこと
二、十字石	✡十字にて六角の石のこと
三、弓	桃の木　矢は鷲の羽のこと　三尺ほどの弓なり
四、剣	将軍木の先に、石刀をつけること
五、槍	将軍木の六尺の先に、石の先あるもの
六、棒	八尺にして将軍木
七、矛矢	三尺の将軍木、棒先槍の如く両端切れるもの
八、矛	槍の両端切れるもの
九、天門、地門	馬で軍略等

右（上訳）尪法という。

後、延元年間、当時より、剣も槍も、武器も、ほとんど近代的となる。」

槍のルールを発見するのに非常に参考になることが書き残されている。

戦国時代、何故に槍術が重要視されたかというと、兜や槍で身を固めた敵に対し、太刀で斬り込んでも深手を負わせることは至難な作業であったが、槍ならば、鎧兜を突き抜き、叩き倒し、払い倒したり、鎧兜の隙間から太刀に比べると、やすやすと突き込むことができるなど、太刀より槍の方が数倍も利点があると悟ったからである。剣の名人と後世に言われた兵法者は、常に戦陣では合理的かつ有効な武器を使用した。飯篠長威斎家直は長刀の名人であり、飯篠若狭守盛信は、神道流槍術の使い手であり、塚原卜伝は弓術と槍の名人である。この卜伝は、本間勘解由左衛門に槍術を伝授している。上野国の一本槍と褒め称えられた上泉伊勢守信綱も、剣法の名人であると共に槍の名人であった。

槍術についての記録を、私の継承した伝書の一部から紹介しよう。この記録を見ると、體術を根本として、そこに槍術が生長し、槍術の名人が生まれたという過程を伺い知ることができる。

神伝不動流打拳體術伝書を見てみると、永久年間神門出雲郷士出雲冠者義照に始まり、正長年間、神門小冠者義兼に於いて尪神不動流打拳體術、剣法、そして槍術の名称が記されている。

本流の水原九郎義成は陸奥水原城主で、義経の落裔という伝説があるが、建久七年頃、打拳體術、馬術、槍術、剣法とも、神伝不動流一剣一閃眼に止まらず、居合の達人だったとも記されている。

たくさんの槍の流派があったが、槍の形状も多彩で、柄の長さは好みによって作

られ、五尺弱の尺槍から、長柄の二間槍、一丈以上の丈寸槍などもあって、手槍、大身槍などと呼ばれ、柄は赤樫や白樫、ビワの木等を用いた。また竹を割いて合わせて柄として槍作りにするもの、長槍といって一丈以上の長い柄づけの槍もあった。

また鉄槍といって、鉄柄のもの、鎌槍といって槍の穂先が鎌状をなしたもの、三本槍、管槍、鉤槍、十字槍もあった。柄のしかけや、穂先の形状について分類することができる。素槍、袋槍、鎌槍、十文字槍、菊地槍、片鎌槍、大身槍等々。

必然的に、槍の形姿と共に、心槍体一如となって、槍術が千変万化の神技を生み、その時代、または後々の語り草により、槍術宗実の継承が生まれ、それが、流宗となったのである。

急所とは

ここで私は、武道で一般的にいわれる急所について書こう。急所というと水月とか喉とか雨戸（首）などのことがあげられるが、鎧兜をつけた場合、急所を覆っているので、斬り突き込めないのが常識となる。急所の字は「九所」「九諸」とも流派によっては書くが、「窮所」というのも急所に対する表現体字となる。

急所は実戦の場合、あるかと思えばなく、ないかと思えばあるものだ。その急所の虚実を知らなければならない。灸点や指圧のつぼの意識と、武道の急所に対する感覚とはまったく異なるものである。「急所を見せる」、これは一つのカウンターともなる。急所を見せて相手の窮所をすべて見る、これも兵法である。

棒術の秘伝、極意の唄に「棒先で虚空を突いて、我が手先に手ごたえあれば、極意なりけり」という一句（虚実）があるように、虚空にある窮所を突くという一字をもって、急所を得んという口伝がある。美空ひばりという歌手がレコーディングする時（これは武芸者の真剣勝負と同じことである）、いつも完璧に歌ったという。それを評して作詞家が言った。「美空ひばりさんは何回唄っても、虚空の中で完璧に唄ってんだな。大空の中で唄うひばりのようにね」と。急所というものを見つけたかったら、このような天性をもちあわせられるように、大空に向かって心を飛ばし、天狗飛切の術や飛鳥の術という槍術との真理を会得して、槍会（柄）一期一会の武風に突きとどめたのである。

太刀と武士道

太刀の長さは、戦国時代の天正年間以来、二尺二寸から長くて二尺三、四寸であった。ちなみに日本人の男性の平均身長は時代や地域によっても異なるが、昔は一般に160センチ（五尺三寸）足らずだったといわれている。元弘年間の名和長年の太刀は四尺三寸（『太平記』）。丹波の人佐治孫五郎、五尺三寸の太刀を帯びる。後村上帝の時、和田正朝の太刀は四尺六寸、藤原康長は四尺八寸の刀を抜くとあ

る。妻鹿孫三郎長宗は五尺三寸。笛吹峠の戦の時、祢津小次郎は六尺三寸の太刀を持つ。赤松氏範は五尺七寸。富樫政親の刀、九尺三寸と講談調の噺（はなし）に出てくる。

忍者刀は、刀身が一尺六寸から七寸のものを用いた。徳川時代、二尺以上を刀と言う。一尺九寸までを大脇差、一尺七寸九分まで中脇差、九寸九分まで小脇差と称した。室町時代からはやりだした打刀（うちがたな）は、はじめ一尺四寸ほどのものだったが、室町時代末期には一尺七、八寸から二尺になった。

大刀と小刀で、大刀を薙刀・槍に換える場合もある。そして大小を併用する。小刀は、また、狭い所で多人数が来て衝突するような場合は効果的である。とくに間合いによいという利点がある。大は小を兼ね、小は大を兼ねる。本当の常識とは、戦うとき、奇眼（きめ）をもって見ることである。奇眼はまた神眼（かなめ）のたとえもあるもので、戦の時には神眼となるもので、とても大切な眼力のことを言う。那須与一が平家の軍扇の要を射落とした故事の秘密は、ここにある。

武器を使おうと思うところに、とらわれが生じる。剣を携えていなくとも、棒を所持していなくとも、いまそこにある物を武器とする。なんでも武器になるものだ。そうした武器の長短、鎧、楯、馬、それらを森羅万象のスクリーンに写して見ることである。時は変れど日本の四季が変ることがないごとく、「武士道は死ぬことと見つけたり」の「詞悌同音の旋律」が、日本の四季が美しいように、武士道における春夏秋冬の美しさを示している。

二の太刀を、一つの太刀、二つの太刀と解すと、大小、または二刀となる。二刀とは二闘とも見えてくる。鎧武者の二の太刀は、闘争の世界へ入る空間である。防囲を突き込む、突き入る手でもある。鎧なき素体の場合、自ずと二の太刀も変化する。二つの太刀は無刀、有刀、真剣にもなる。

剣、薙刀、槍も時代によって変化がある。新陰流の伝書『天狗書秘伝之巻』に、一、乱勝　一、鈎旭　一、雲截　一、電光、という流技名と、大小二本の竹刀をもって闘う絵が残されている。武風を知らぬものは、ここから宮本武蔵の二刀流の大刀と小刀の姿を思い出すに違いない。上泉武蔵守は、そんな感覚しかない武芸者を一笑し、そして諭すであろう。「この竹刀の大小の絵には、片手に太刀、片手に槍か薙刀また長刀（ながまき）を描くのじゃ、その秘めたる図示なのじゃ、秘画じゃがのう。おわかりか……後の世では、『天狗芸術論』なんぞいう文章を発表する人もいるが……ま、それはそれとして、太刀をもって闘いぬいた時代を知らぬものは、気の毒なことじゃ」と。要は、小太刀は小太刀だけにあらず。鎧通し、槍の穂先、薙刀の刃身も同じなりと勘ずることにある。十方折衝の虎擲龍挐（こてきりょうだ）の図の修羅場を見られたし。

第3章　武道修行

極意と変化

　極意というものは最高のものと思いがちであるが、これは、その人、その人の主観、その時の「主勘」によって、異質なものに変化する。そこに気づかないと、極意がスポーツ感覚でいう得意技に等しいものとなり、かえって死を呼ぶことになってしまう。そこで極意というものは、陰と陽とが引き合っているという現象から始まると知ることが大切である。この現象を知って、陰の力、引力の自然体の優理性、その本体を悟り、流派の極意として、「極意とは」と解き始めている。

　得意技はまた「天狗技」といって戒めたものだ『天狗芸術論』である。

　江戸時代、関宿藩の藩士だった佚斎樗山子の『天狗芸術論』という、天狗が武道の極意を語る内容の本がある。高松先生は言われていた。「人間は天狗になるやさかいな。でも天狗になるって大事なんや。その中から名人が出るんやさかい」と。人生においては、ある時期は天狗でもいい。そうした血気盛んな時期も必要なのだろう。闘いとは男の武器、女の武器、その様も最大限に駆使するものであるからだ。そこには両性ともに良勢の気がある。とはいえ、天狗が高じて一方的な転愚にならぬこと。色欲に溺れるもの術力失うなり。

　『天狗芸術論』とか『猫の妙術』といった、いわゆる武道についての本を読むときは、本にとりつかれぬようにしなさい、と私は言いたい。天狗は転愚になる字変があるとか、窮鼠猫を嚙む、猫もねずみに負けることがあるのだと単純に思ったりすることが大切だ。書物には洗脳する力があると承知したいものである。天狗が男性的というならば、猫は女性的なものという見地（剣血）から見るのも一興である。

　私が旧制中学生の頃の、おもしろい話がある。悪ガキだった私たちを「お前たちは勉強の仕方がわかっとらん。飯を食って糞をたれるだけ。製糞機みたいなものだ」と先生に叱られた。なるほど、書物が燃やされてしまう焚書という行為もそこにつながってくる。言うなれば、金魚のうんこということになる。本を読むことで、くだらぬ知識にとどまるな、またとらわれるなと私は言いたい。武士道を知ることのできる名著といわれる山本常朝の「葉隠」にしても、彼は武士であったか、そして武道をどの程度修行したかを知ることが大切であり、そこから読書を出発させなければならない。

　さて神社の社殿などに、よく狛犬が向かい合わせに置かれているが、この狛犬は別名、戻り獅子、向かい獅子と言う。ある日、一匹が宝庫から盗まれた。盗まれなかった一匹があくる夜より夜泣きをするようになり、困っていたが、盗まれた獅子を取り返した晩から、不思議にも夜泣きが停まった。その噂を聞いた高僧が、この二匹の獅子を祀り、祈願をかけると、霊験あらたかで、やがて相別れ、相離れたものを元に返す祈願像になったという。師の高松先生も、祈願しながら、この戻り獅子、向かい獅子をお造りになられたと聞いている。

　地水火風空の五編から成る宮本武蔵の『五輪書』を読むとき、ＣＤの中からジャズのサウンド「テイクファイヴ」を選び出して聞いていると、一気に読めるよ、と私は読書好きに語っている。キャラバカア。天韻地水火風空の五線譜から武韻を聞く。その後、紙に向かい、武道・剣法の絵を描く。

　武闘から武芸へ、そして武士道という道を歩み、その道は陸、海、空の参道へと映像化され、サムライという映画が上映されては消えて行く。迷いの脳裏に止まるのみと槍の達人・高橋泥舟の描いた骸骨が笑っている。

　残心とは、表技で表現すれば、残心的解釈でよいだろうが、裏技でその音を聞いたとき、その山響きは斬新という音になって帰ってくるのである。このように武道の音の表裏を聞き分けられないようでは、残心の心構えは生じてこない。武道の実践の残心とは、斬進に一転するネクストワンの間にある。見えぬ、見切る、見届ける、その響きまでも聞かねばならぬ。そして諸行無常の音、鐘の音を、聞かぬうちに自覚することである。

　宮本武蔵の二天一流、その二天とは、人が生々流転し、二転三転とする、その変化する流れを示したものである。自然は美しいからこそ変化する。変化するから美しい。とはいえ、その変化が正常でないと、大災害がそこに待ち受けている。世も二転三転して、洪水によって肥沃な土地が残り、燃えた大地の焼け跡に種子が生き残り、花を咲かせて三転するのである。

大小と心技体

『一寸法師』という有名な昔話がある。一寸法師は生まれて何年経っても、大人の小指ほどの大きさしかなかったが、とても元気だった。都へ行って侍になる夢を抱き、お椀の船に乗って、川を下り、京の都にたどり着いた。立派な武家に仕えることを許され、姫君が清水寺にお参りしたおり、乱暴者の大きな鬼が襲ってきたが、ただひとりで姫を守って、鬼を退治する。その鬼の残した打ち出の小槌を振ると、法師はみるみる大きくなり、りっぱな若者になったという話である。

　武道家といえば、柔道の三船久蔵先生、合気道の植芝盛平先生、空手の船越義珍先生といった人物がすぐに頭に浮かぶ。三氏とも背の低い方で、体が小さいからバランスが良かったということと同時に、人一倍修行を重ねているうちに、武芸の成長とともに器が大きくなり、名人となった。その前に出ると、自分よりずっと大きく見えたという印象を多くの人が語っている。刀に大小があるように、人間の体にも大きい人、小さい人がいる。しかし心技体の成長が大小を能とする。大は小を兼ねる。自分の価値観を知る者にとっては武風に寸法なし、ということである。

師と弟子

　高松先生は武号を一時、澄水とし、澄水のような心を大切にされていた。この武号は、「水清ければ魚棲まず」という諺と重なってくる。師はこの澄水の流れ、大自然の神泉を大切にされたのである。この神泉の流れに住むことに反する魚、いうなれば武道家としての自覚を失ったものは、武道の道を失うのである。

　「三尺下がって師の影を踏まず」という諺がある。一般の人はそこに、師弟間の弟子としての心構えしか受け入れていないようだが、師というものは、弟子の三尺先に立ち、敵の攻撃を自ら影楯となって実は弟子を守っているのだということに気づいている人が、はたしてどれだけいるだろうか。しかも師とはさらに伝統をも護ってきた。先に立って未来を見ているのである。

　私は師の影を踏まないような心で修行し続けてきたのだが、弟子を育て導くようなことを四五十年も続けて、ふと気づくことがあった。それは影の本体、師そのものの姿である。影を踏まず、そんなことを考えているうちは師のお心なぞわからぬものである。師と同じ年齢も過ぎた今、師というものは弟子を護るため先を見て導いていなくてはならないのだと気づいたのである。良い弟子ばかりでなく、弟子にあるまじき弟子に遭遇することがあっても、それを守る。私は「師匠」を「示正」とも書こう。高松先生が言われた愛深き言葉の数々と、「初見さんを愛門人にいたしましょう」と書かれた一枚の葉書が想い出される。

　命というのは不思議なもので、いい師匠といい弟子がいれば、それを継続していくことができる。師匠に匹敵する大きな器の弟子が選ばれ、その道の器に入った水をこぼさぬよう継承していく。高松先生からいただいた書に「我無し」という言葉が書いてあった。この「我」だが、方言によっては相手を指す言葉であるということに気づかないと、師と話が通じなくなる。即ち「我無し」とは相手無しとも、敵無しとも聞けるからである。とはいえ、師弟の間に下克上が生じる時もある。しかし清い流れだけがいつまでも澄水生命水に生き続けている。

　師匠と弟子についていえば、上泉伊勢守ほど名ある弟子を持ったものはあるまい。疋田文五郎、神後伊豆、奥山休賀斎、丸目蔵人、柳生宗厳、松田織部之助、那河彌左エ門、足利義輝、豊臣秀次、これら名だたる人々の顔ぶれを見てもうなずけることであろう。柳生宗厳は後に但馬入道石舟斎宗厳と称した。入道したので、法名を宗厳、斎名を石舟斎と言った。宗矩は石舟斎の五男である。

　百人一首のカルタのように、武道や生活における極意の歌を集めた「××百首」といったものがあり、それを見ると楽しくなってくる。歌には伝承の意味があって、そこから秘伝を見抜いていくことができるからだ。百首には敵の百の首という意味があるのかもしれない。首とは「九秘」「久秘」の象徴でもあろう。首は主の同音である。「主よ導き給え、助け給え」の福音を首が発す、その音合わせなのだろうか。宗厳も『新陰百首』を書いて残しているが、筆者は塚原卜伝の『卜伝百首』の本を所有している。このほか『義盛百首』『宝蔵院百首』『妖怪百首』なども

あり、百鬼夜行百物語はお百度参りの祈りにも似ている。

伝承と虚実のあいだ

　伝承と虚実、それは伝承と今日、そこに実が存在していることが大切である。近頃私は、伝承とは宇宙体の生命につながっているのだなあ、と思うようになった。例えば世襲とは、親子でなくとも、宇宙体と結ばれている人間同志が、縁あって結ばれて、伝承し生き続けているものだと定義づけている。そうした世襲なくして、やがて伝承されるということがあるだろうか。武道の伝書にはよく、継承者の間に「何代略」と記されている。これもその一例であろう。伝承の虚とは、虚でないということであり、継承者は常に実体となって表れてくるものだ。結婚して数年経ち、子供のできない私たち夫婦に対して、高松先生はこうおっしゃられたものだ。「ほんまの子やなくてもな、愛情やさかいな」と。伝承と虚実、そこには愛情の他に何も必要としないのである。

　歌舞伎には伝承の型がある。江戸はきっちりとした型の伝承を美徳とし、上方は型よりも伝承者の内面の表現力を美徳としている。ここに型の命を伝える虚実がある。歌舞伎役者、市川団十郎の舞台話を二つ紹介しよう。

　その一。市川団十郎が毎日劇中で布団に座る場面があって、裏方が座る場所に布団を置く仕事を命じられた。ところが、舞台がはねた後、団十郎は毎日のように、布団の置き方が悪いとなじる。そこで、殴られなかったある日、布団を置いた場所に印をつけて、もしこれでも明日市川団十郎に殴られるようだったら、刺し違えて死んでやる、と懐に短刀を潜ませて舞台の終幕を待った。ところが当日は殴られなかった。裏方ははたと気づき、団十郎に手をついて詫びた。「申し訳ございません。私はお師匠様の芸の適確な動きも見ることができず、本当に未熟者でした。ほとほと恥じ入っております。私はお師匠様を殺そうと想った瞬間がありました。何とぞ存分にご成敗下さい」と。団十郎、「そうか。主がいったように、私も命をかけて芝居をしているんだ。気にするな」と答えたという。

　その二。団十郎の立廻りのシーンで剣道の心得のあるものが、隙があったら斬り込もう、と想ったが、一分の隙もなし。剣の道の師匠でもあると尊敬したという。

　この二つのエピソードは、型の組み合わせにも隙間がないということを物語っている。一見、様式美の世界から「要識秘」の世界を見てとることができるのである。

明日への武道

「道場での稽古は、一言でどう言い表せるでしょうか」と尋ねられて、こう答えたことがある。「そうだね、道場とはプールみたいなもの。泳げない人を泳ぎができ

るようにすることから始めるようなものだね。人生をプールするものですね」。

「風姿花伝」について前述したが、わが師・高松先生は花性竹性といって、その心意気の一つである花を愛された。「花」の字は草が化けると書く。その生命力の強さを花や草に喩えたのだろう。花は切ってもまた咲く。枯れたり姿がなくなっても、種が芽吹いたり根が残っていて、翌年には咲く花も少なくない。すなわち命である。古代には人を尊んで何々の命と名づけた。

武芸者である私は、武道の志のある者たちに一事で武道の本質を知らしめるべく、過去の魂に遡っている。これまで命を落としていたかもしれないような機会が何度もあったが、いまも元気で過ごしているのは、やはり使命があったのだろう。そして先生の三十三回忌を迎えたので、そうした魂の武道の公開に踏み切った。何事も人間同士の魂と魂の触れ合いが一番大事なのである。世界中に、日本の武道の種をまいておけば、それがどこかで成長し存続するかもしれないと思っている。

私には世界に武道を教えに行くとか、広めようという考えは毛頭なかった。ただ、世界が武道を見ている目が、私の目とまったく違うのに唖然とした。当時、私は若さの「若勘」を生かし、武道を知らせなければならぬという血気が、私に世界に走らせた。ようやく世界の人々の「勘化」を見て、世界の旅から着陸し、2004年からは旅に出ないことにした。

高松先生との出逢いから、武風一貫して四十八年。相撲の四十八手ではないが、武芸の四十八数が見えるようになってきた。この間、身技体に関して、ひとつとして同じようなことをした覚えがない。玉虎流天略の巻でいう「万化」である。宇宙はたえず変化している。我もまた宇宙の稽古に出場しているということである。宇宙のすべては万有引力で引き合っている。時間と空間、そして過去と現在と未来は互いに密接に結びつけられている。いまや私はタイムスリップしている。五山文学の世界、そして俳聖・芭蕉が詠んだ「夏草や兵どもが夢の跡」の奥の細道も歩いている。

武神館道場の武道體術の最高段位は十五段である。そこで頂点だと思う人がいるが、高い山も虚空に立っているから美しいのである。玉虎流の秘伝書に、上略、中略、下略に分けて、秘技が記されている。その秘伝書の始めにある虚空の一手はスタートの秘技とされている。

いま武神館道場は世界的に伝播され、武道家の心を会得し、十五段位に結ばれた武道家たちが成長している。その彼等が言う。「十五段になって思います。日本では侍が十五歳で元服して大人になる儀式があるそうです。僕達も、十五歳の大人になれたのですね」と。本書は、武道家として元服式に出席できる心得の書として読んでいただきたいと願いつつ、尽力に筆力を加えたしだいである。

TECHNICAL TEXT

武士の心得

武士道とは、次の文で味わうことで武士道に光をともす。

「武士の心得として起居動作、則ち礼儀を慎み人道を過たざるを武風という。粗忽尾籠の振る舞なきように、また軽率に流れず、悠揚迫らず、厳然臆せず、慎み深く、慈愛に富み、最も武勇を尊重するは申すまでも無し。然りと雖も血気に委せて乱暴狼藉にならぬよう、要武風の深く戒める所なり。

弱者を扶け強者を挫くと雖も、猥りに争う事は許さず。やむを得ぬ場合、強きをも恐れず弱者を扶けてこそ、真の武人というべきである。恥辱を与える者あれども、笑って相手せざる勇が真の勇なり。同時に、猥りに刀に手をかけること、絶対に慎むべし。則ち、秋霜烈日の如き勇気果断の気象に伴うに、春風駘蕩たる慈愛の徳と共に、優雅なる心を保持し、文武を貴び、文弱に流るる事なく、一方的に片寄らず、武勇と共に優しき心を知るを真の武神と人がいう。これ武人の常の心得と誓うべし。」

礼　武道の起居動作は、礼によって礼に始まるが、武士の礼とは仁義礼智信という言葉の中にある。礼はその中心にあって、要となるものであり、かつまたバランスを自覚するものであると知ることが大切である。これを悟れば、おのずから武士道という道からはずれることがない。

組太刀　組討ち、組太刀、それは無刀、太刀、長器と一如の対戦感覚を養うことである。そこには常に體術が原動力となって存在しているが故に、一妙の體術と太刀が命となり、秘剣の構を見せるのである。

位取りといって、構にも位がある。その武士の位によって、おのずから構えに人間性、即ち素晴らしさとか畏（かしこ）しさなどがにじみ出てくる。それは形から生まれるものではない。

無刀捕り秘伝　無刀捕りというと、自分は刀をもたず、相手は刀を持っているものだと思う人が多いが、そうではない。自分が刀を持っていても、無刀の心構えで相手に対応できる度胸を養うことに始まるのである。それには體術を充分に修練しておかなければ、無刀捕りの妙技を会得することが出来ない。そのためには修業の道の目的をまず知ることである。剣は、斬ること、突くことだけに片寄って修業していくと、知らず知らずに邪剣の道へ進むことになる恐れがある。人を生かすための剣、剣生（けんせい）、すなわち、剣聖の道に生きることが出来ず、剣を斬るためだけの道愚とし、生涯を骸骨のごとき姿で生きることになるのである。

武人の心とは、心の構を支配する、自然の心が肝心（神心）である。武人の體の構えを支配するのも心なのである。故に、精神と身體を一致しなくては武道家としての要をなさない。この一致した心構え、そこには隙がないのである。相手が吾を

斬らんとする構えを見せたところで、相手の剣は、我には一寸たりとも触れること
はできぬ。わが気合で、忽ち倒れるぞという気迫、そして沈勇の姿、それは神妙心
の聖姿なのである。そこに敵の攻勢、わが気迫に包まれて不動金縛りとなり、一
喝、遠当の術にも倒されるのである。この決意なくして無刀捕りの極意は得られな
いということを知って錬磨することである。

　ここで無刀捕りの稽古、または真剣型について述べておこう。無刀捕りという
と、刀の攻撃に対する心構と早合点する人が多いが、槍、薙刀、弓、手裏剣、銃に
対する武闘捕りの風姿であるということを知っていただきたい。ここに万変不驚と
いう一悟を心とし、万化に対する武闘捕りを心得とし、風天護身、龍虎闘う時、雲
を呼び、雨を呼び、暗雲来るを、心念で風を呼び、吹き飛ばし、円光に見ることが
できるのである。しかるに反応汎溢の十字の構は、洪水の勢いに溢れるに似て、敵
<ruby>はんのうばんえつ</ruby>
勢を一気に流し消し去るのである。

隼雄　敵が大刀を抜かんとす。我は隼のごとく敵の刀の柄頭を左手で押える。敵は
一歩引いて抜かんとす。我は忽ち右手親指で敵の鼻下を突く（敵はアッと言って離
す）。忽ち柄を右手に持って一歩引くのと同時に、わが方に刀を抜き、左手刀身に
そえて突きの構え。残心（斬進、残心）。

　隼人打ち。突きは切っ先だけにあらず。柄頭、鍔すべてはこれ突きと一体と化
す。

隼足　敵が大刀を抜かんとす。我は左手で前のごとく柄頭を押える。敵が右手でわ
が左手首を打つ。我は忽ち敵の左側に身を転じ、右手で刀の後鞘を持ち、左手で敵
の左手首を持ち右手を上げると、ちょうど敵の左手を刀の鞘で押える。刀の柄は敵
の左足を囲むこととなる。敵は俯向けに倒れ、刀で押えられる。忽ち右足にて蹴込
んで倒し、押え捕える。

一撃　敵が大上段に構える。我は忽ち左手で敵の右肘を押えると同時に、右手親指
で敵の胸部を突き当て、右足で蹴上げると、敵は仰向けに倒れる。忽ち右足で敵の
右足横を蹴り突く。鎧武者胸部とは境武という。

魁足　敵が大上段で斬り込みくる。我は体を左に転じてかわすと、敵の一刀が右横
に流れ、刀は飛ぶ。忽ち右足で敵の右手を蹴上げる。敵は小刀に手をかける。我は
手刀で敵の右を霞打ち。敵がひるみ仰向けに倒れる。忽ち敵右腕の中関節を左手で
持ち、右大外のごとくして敵を跳ね上げる。残心。

拘掠　敵が大上段で斬り込みくる。我は体を右足によけてかわすと、敵の大刀が左
側に流れる。忽ち左手で敵の右手首をつかむ。同時に右手で敵の右腕中関節を掴む
や、我が両足とも、俯向けに倒れかける敵の右横に流し、捨身となって忽ち起きて
残心。一刀を持つも持たぬも同じ動き。

意合封　敵が右横薙ぎに斬り込みくる。我は一歩後方に飛びのく。敵は再び大上
段。我は忽ち飛込んで左腕受身の形となり、右親指を敵の左胸に当て込み、忽ち右
足にて蹴倒す。退いて残心。親指とは鎧通し槍打振等なり。

沈雁　敵は青眼に構える。我は汎溢の構。忽ち正面から突き来る。我は体を沈めて左に転ずると、敵の一刀は右に流れる。左手で敵の右手首を打ち摑む。忽ち右手を添え体を沈めて、敵の刀を持つ手をわが頭上より左へ回し、左足を引き坐す。右足蹴当て。敵は仰向けに倒れる。残心。蹴当とは気当てなり。

風盃　敵が大上段で斬り込みくる。我は左に体を転じ、右手で敵の鍔前に刀身を押え、鍔上を指先で持つ。忽ち左手刀で敵の顔面に飛び、同時に刀を引き捕る。これを真剣捕りとも言う。捕った一刀を左手で持つなり横薙ぎに斬り倒す。打ち倒すなり。

無刀捕り・意合捕り胴返し

柄隠れの一刀　柄の中に短刀が仕込んである。これにて投げ、突きなど、十方折衝の體術の術と閃化する。指刀突きなり。

瓊躯＝抜く　刀を抜く時、鍔に親指をかけて、抜き始めの風姿とするのが一般にいう「鯉口を切る」ことだが、この風姿では、親指とは陰の指といって、示指、指環拳で切る。前腕、肘、体を使って、左右の手で抜く。この鯉口を切る法は、鯉の瀧登りの一語に似て、昇鯉、すなわち勝利への抜刀法とは、陰陽の引き合う現象であると知ることが肝心である。この現象を悟った者が、影流の本体を知ることが出来るのである。そして居合抜刀道を見る。この鍔は、直木三十五が、作品を記念して、作品名を鍔に彫り込んだものである。

天地人の構　秋田の剣豪・小野岡隆俊は剣を天地人に構えることを特徴とした。右耳の辺りに刀身の鍔先九寸左前方斜めに位取る。左足を引けば、勢い強く相手方の左胴に入る。たとえ相手方の剣が先に斬り込みくるとも、忽ちこれを払い斬りにしたという。また右足を引けば勢い強く左面に斬り込むという剣である。

突　切先で制する。気先でもある。写真を見ればわかるように、相手の小手すべての体勢を包み込んでいる。

小手　一閃と観じとれば剣千手（三十三間堂の千手観音像）の韻が聞こえてくる。帯刀とは雄秘留ことである。

護身体　大刀、小刀にても同じく帯びることが大切なり。刀を我に刺すに同じなり。太刀をさし後方に廻し下緒をたすきとす。抜く刀、抜くことあたわず禁。対手の太刀の柄をいただき流水のまま八刀に変化、抜き構える。抜きながら八方に変化、九字を祈って気を振う。

八法秘剣

一、軍略　天門　地門

二、杖術　及び半棒術

三、六尺棒　及び体の位取

四、薙刀　眉尖刀術

五、小太刀　及び十手術

六、騎射　及び水術

七、手裏剣　及び銛盤投げ術

八、槍術

九、秘剣

　秘剣術とは體術剣法のことを言い、八法に秘剣術を加えて九法とする、武士の心得を総証（総称）したものである。體術を必勝の術として、骨指術、骨法術、柔體術、打拳體術、忍法體術との呼び名が生まれ、そこに秘剣術の流命が生じたのである。わが八方秘剣の術にては剣を斜地釣正眼という。相手が斬り込み来たらば忽ち斬る構である。右足を己の肩幅ほど後ろに引く。例えば相手方が突き、または胴に斬り込み来るならば、忽ち小手を返し相手の剣を払い飛ばす。この呼吸を悟り、虚実を用いたのが佐々木小次郎のつばめ斬りである。

附込　正眼の構。敵は大上段。わが正眼は一心に敵の胸板を目差し、眼は敵の眼を見つめる。敵の大上段など一切気に止めず、敵の斬り込まんとする一利那に気合を掛ける。敵がひるむと同時に右足を出し、左足は坐し突き。

　附込という技は、鎧を着用している時、または、相手が武器や楯とするものをもつ、または楯とするものがある場合は一変する。ここに"突く"というだけで、突く場所が書いていないところに心伝口伝がある。突き込めば、かならずそこには変化がある。そこに附込もって突き込む所に、生命閃、死尖が生まれる。この尖の一時を戦という一字で覚えさせるので、體術が附込をもって、鎧通しで突き込む、あるいは太刀で突き込む。ここで左足を坐すということは、不動座、心の不動、心のすわった、心念の姿を指すものである。

左右逆　三本あり。この構は一の構、即ち剣はわが顔面に真直ぐに立て直立のこと。敵が大上段で斬り込みくれば、左右どちらでも撥ね返しやすく、右に撥ねれば小手返し。敵の右首を左に撥ねれば小手を返し、左肩に体を転ずれば真二つに斬り込む。

　一の構。まず一という帰一する数位の理を知ることである。禅でいう、⊖の接待の頓である。左右逆とは、虚実陰陽の逆である。この逆をギャグと思ってほしい。ギャグはアドリブから生まれることがあるように、熟練したところから生ずる。小手、これは、手首や前腕の斬り所と思う人があるが、そうではなく、小さい、見えにくい、変化、技と思ってほしい。真二つに斬り込むということは、左右逆の動きの中で、隙を見た旬間、その旬という気を見ること、それが秘なのである。

突掛　青眼の構。敵は大上段、我は突きに出るとすれば、敵が斬り下すとき相打ちとなる。故にこの突きは右足を出し左足は坐す。これにおいて一瞬わが突きが早く、敵がこの突きをかわすとすれば、忽ち小手を返し、右胴に斬り込むなり。

　相手に斬らせたと思う体変術の錬磨が威彩を放つ。相手の斬るという心を挫打させる雲と水の関係を相手に斬らせる。その空間に光を放ち、瞬間、小手を返し、左胴。しかし鎧を着用の場合、わが突きの風姿は楯のごとく、身楯一転、右胴に斬り掛かる。この掛かるという字をよくかみしめていただきたい。右胴に斬り掛かっ

て、そこからの変化が秘伝なのである。斬り掛かる戦乱の映像を自分の脳裏に映していただきたい。

左右逆　三本あり。下段の構で一度敵の面上高く剣を上げることは敵をまどわす。虚忽ち小手返し。実は右胴または小手返し、左胴または突きの一手なり。

　これは、掛、左右逆と思ってみてほしい。相手の面上、兜に当てても斬り込めず。しかしこの時、我は不動心で相手を迷わす、心技の太刀打ちとす。兜は斬れずとも、敵の心を打ちのめす心意気、組討ちの心意気である。太刀の小手、組討ちなる故に大技は使わず、太刀体、柄、鎧も含むと共に、相手の右胴、左胴、左右から、打ち太刀、突き太刀、倒し、討ち取るなり。

斬上　中段の構。敵は大上段。敵がまさに斬り下す一瞬、先に小手を返し、右脇より左肩に向けて斬り上げる。この時敵も斬り下したとすれば、敵の一刀を撥ね上げることとなり、忽ち小手返し、突きに出る。中段斬上返しという。

　剣、太刀、刀にてもそうだが、これは無刀、小太刀、大太刀と思ってみてほしい。兜割りかもしれない。相手の斬り込みは、一刀と限らず、長巻等の長刀や、遠心力の強い斬り込みと思ってもよく、これを避ける、避けない瞬間をおのずから作る。それは風力、あるいは風の力といってもよいだろう。故に武風一貫という事柄を大切にするのである。この句を見て、相手の心技体から来たる一刀を跳ね上げる。わが心技體術、心技体力が相手の剣刀を跳ね上げるのだ。その瞬間、相手の右胴に、押え突き、小手を返し、體も転変し、右胴に突き上げる。鎧着用の者に対し、斬り上げること、「勇利」なり。

左右逆　三本あり。天地人の構。真正面を向き、剣は右耳の辺りに真直ぐ立てる。上半身は右斜め向き。敵は大上段より斬り込みくる。右足を一歩引く。忽ち敵の左胴から斬り上げ、左足を引きかわせば逆右下より斜め上に斬り上げる。

　これは、相手の斬り込む決死なる體の攻撃に対して、それを引き流すような気力をもって、右足の宙心力を利して、相手の左胴をぶつ斬りに叩き斬り上げるものである。交激心または左足を中心力とすれば、相手の右下より吹き上げる山嵐に見る風力と和すことを念じ、斬り上げる。秘剣と変化させるのである。

斬下　天地の構。敵は真正面。剣を正面に立てる。敵が大上段より斬り下しくる。左足を引いて受け、敵が進みきたらば鍔ぜりとなるが、ぐっと押して刀の切っ先を左に下げて右側に体を転じ、敵を左肩先より斬り下げる。この空間でわが肘、前腕を支点に変化、太刀尖刀にて斬り下げ。

　相手の斬り下げを捕手のごとくいなし、真正面より受けるごとくせず、あくまでも、受け捕を引き変ずるごとく、体変し、斬り下げる。これは刀体を「優閃」し押し斬り、次の変体によって、深手を使うことにある。

左右逆　三本あり。天地の構。左側に体を転じ、右脇より斬り上げる。鍔ぜりとなり右足にて蹴り上げ、突きの一手なり。

　蹴り上げ、相手の體に応じ、蹴り下げた足力に応じ、隙に当て突き入る一手。一

手とは、始めなり。

鎹止 下段の構。敵は大上段、我は下段の構から右へ右へと姿勢を転じる。敵も自然体を転ずる。忽ち気合と共に左足を引いて、一刀を中段上段と転ず。斬り込むと右側に一転、敵の左上より小手に斬り込む。

　鎹止により今までの口伝を参考にして修業会得することで、敵を見るより己を正すことにより、相手の術は破れを生ずるという。自然体、自然の心を秘とすることである。自然とは、師曰く、誠の精神にありという。

左右逆 三本あり。前の通り小手を斬り上げるのと突きに転ずるのとがあり。重ねて言う。小手とは小さな術間を近く斬り差げるなり。

小蝶返 大上段の構。敵は青眼、我は右足を後斜めに引き、素早く右へ転ずる。大上段のまま小蝶のごとく軽く右に転ずると同時に小手に斬り込む。小蝶斬りともいう。また敵の剛力勢を戯れとする霞の蝶のごとき動勢力を保つ法なり。

左右逆 三本あり。右に転じ、敵の左肩に斬り付ける。または突きに転ずる等なり（口伝）。

四方斬 天地八相の構。右斜めの姿勢。敵の左胴を逆斬りに斬り小手返し。敵の右胴に斬り返し、忽ち突きに入る（口伝）。

左右逆 三本あり。最後の突きが真向二つ割に出る。または逆裾払い（口伝）。

八方斬 天地八相の構。この技も捨身という。八相より敵の左脇を斬り下げ、体を右に充分に転じ左脇を斬り下げ、次も忽ち右へ転じ、同じく斬り下げる。

左右逆 三本あり。左技あり、真向竹割あり（口伝）。

月之輪 青眼の構。この構は真一文字に敵の首に突き入れるなり。秘転の突きともいう。首とは百歌にあり。百人一首の意を味わわれたし。

左右逆 三本あり。脇腹に突き入れる。また腹部に突き入るのもあり。

生々流転その剣法 各流秘剣も、前記の心構えを秘とすることを前提としていたと知っていただきたい。

柳生流青眼の構 有名な柳生流が特徴とするのは青眼直立である。自分の肩幅ほど開き、剣先は相手方の眼につける。青眼に構えることは自然の体勢であり、

一、相手方はこの剣先が邪魔になって斬り込みにくい。

二、相手方が斬り込んできても、左右後ろに剣をかわすことができる。

三、同時に相手方の隙に斬り込みやすい。

という三つの利点があるからだ。

下段の構 陸前に井鳥巨雲為信という剣豪あり。弘流と称す。その特徴は剣を下段に構える。これは相手の剣の打ち込みを待っている構で、相手方が胴にても面にても斬り込み来らんとき、剣を払い上げ飛ばし、その隙に斬り込むという。

甲冑太刀

甲冑剣法 敵大上段打ち太刀を肩衣にとる。一の太刀を肩衣のまま捕る。一の太刀突き込み。二の太刀、首輪に斬り裂く。

陣中の平の構。槍突きを跳ね上げて入身。槍手を捕り上げ太刀にて小手捕りに行きつつ入身。要所太刀入身。

組討太刀武二武惨（ぶにむざん）。組討太刀。要捕り要入り神眼。神眼を要（かなめ）と呼ぶ。要討ち捕る。

肩車にかつぎ山嵐にかつぎ飛ばし。甲冑武者をかつぎ上げる。百石かつぎともいう。墜落する武者、雪崩のごとく岩砕きのごとく突武死（つぶし）討ち捕る。

戦陣二天の構より二天討ち。一の太刀で敵の攻め手を打つ。二の槍を突き込みつつ敵の太刀を落し、我が右足にて槍を踏む。太刀を捕りつつ蹴込み、敵の要所を太刀にて討ち取る。槍は鎧姿の相手の隙を突きやすい。その優位性のため、戦場では槍を用いて戦う時代があった。

太刀討　八双に打ち込む体勢を右手捕り。右太刀を左胴に叩き倒す体勢にて討ち叩く。入体変々。敵刀を左兜に左上腕肩にて鎧體上げ込み、右太刀突き入り押え。太刀を左手に持ち替えて鎧通しにて突き込み、握柄より押し倒す勢いで首も斬る。

敵多数。太刀射一如。敵の射勢を我が鎧體変岩動のごとし。彼我六刀即ち太刀三鎧通し三我がものとす。突き入れ。これ手呼（梃子）體動という自然の勝利なり。

殿中衣装　ナンバ歩きは長袴を着ければわかる。「浮舟のごとし」を無刀の心得とする。波静かなればよく高からばよし。

飛鳥の剣来たるを自然とす忍。二天一刀二天一流とする。生位に浮舟にのり敵飛騰を止める。浮舟の動要に敵動くあたわず。

獅子撃　我小刀中正眼。長袴、猛虎一声にして響く。敵斬り込みに双吼の気合いにて一歩前進。虚空を乱し敵無敵の位に。避け裂けの和韻を発し、小刀猛虎の牙爪巨体と化し威圧する。

十字剣　我は両手を下げたまま音無しの構。強敵来るとも、この様。木火土金水五行中の四行を水の勢いにて四行を十字となし、我が水の帥位（すいい）は大自然と化し結ぶ。十字を結し（決死）捨手味十字剣の極意を生ず。

師・高松寿嗣先生、その八方秘剣　心妙剣／遠撃渕。三引之大手／遠撃渕。独楽弾きの一手。飛倒竹割りの一手。燕返しの一手／心妙不動之剣／玉手斬り変化。斬り返し。絡捕り。不動之剣勢陰陽。遠撃渕の剣勢虚実。心妙剣三才の剣勢天地人を斬る／秘勝心妙剣。十二天法燕返し。

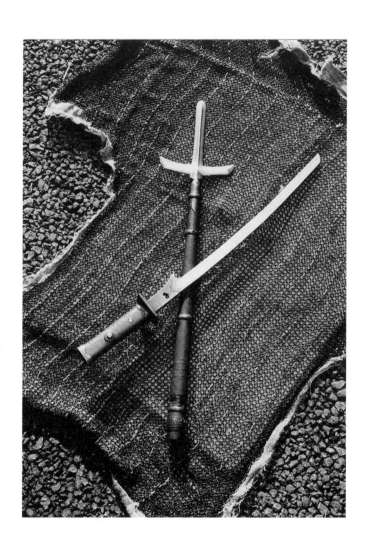